A GHOST
WITHOUT
A LIFE

Corinne Edwards
Paul Van Name

Chicago, IL.

By Corinne Edwards and Paul Van Name

ISBN-13:
978-1500570217

ISBN-10:
1500570214

Author's note
This book is fiction with a few references to actual experiences..
In those cases, the names and details have been changed to protect the privacy of the people involved.

Some material is taken from *Reflections from a Woman Alone and A Man Without a Woman by Corinne Edwards*

This book is dedicated with love and gratitude —
to my wonderful sons, Mark, Paul, Peter and
Alexander,
their beautiful wives —
Karen, Rain and Dawn,

and my exceptional grandchildren,
Veronica, Julius II and Mylana Rose —

To Julie, Sheila, Dee, Pat, Arlene, Stevie, Jamie,
And my mother, Helen Coryat -
wherever they are —

and to my beloved brother, Henry and best
friend and sister, June.

Chapter One

An older four door Lincoln is pulling into a parking lot, in heavy rain, under a sign which reads *Michaelson's Funeral Home*. The car backfires as it is parked. Two women open umbrellas, exit the car and run toward the doorway.

My husband, Julius is gone. We were married for 20 years. He was always difficult but the last five years when he was so sick were really hard. For him - and for me.

He was a stockbroker with a large firm. I joined the company a few years after I graduated from college. My parents were gone so I decided to stay in Chicago.

I did not know Julius except for a few "Good Mornings" in the elevator.

I loved working there for a group of brokers. I even got qualified by taking the test to be a broker myself. I didn't do any trading but it gave me a greater understanding of how things were done.

I had a nickname. They called me "Minnesota Nice." I had grown up on a farm in Minnesota.

Julius was one of the successful stars there. I used to hear that he was one of the most eligible men in Chicago.

He was handsome, charming and you could not help but notice his beautiful custom suits, shirts and handmade shoes from London. He always drove the latest luxury sports car and had a cruiser on Lake Michigan. Rumor had it that he employed a Japanese house boy to take care of his beautiful apartment and his errands.

Julius had an assistant, Alice, who had been with him for years. It was said that she was the only one who could handle him since he could be demanding and difficult at times.

Suddenly, Alice had a medical crisis and would be out on leave for three to six months. He needed a temporary assistant. The HR department looked around and I was one of the women chosen to be interviewed.

I was scared. He was very direct.
He started out by telling me he was impressed that I had graduated Summa Cum Laude from Northwestern.
"Does that mean you are smart?" I said. "Yes."
"Can you work under pressure?" I again said. "Yes."
Your nickname, I hear is "Minnesota Nice." That scares me a little. Can you be tough also?" Again, I answered. "Yes, if I had to."
"OK. You'll start Monday."
"One last thing. My work is confidential. You will have to limit your contact with your previous brokers." I agreed.
Things went well. He was very complimentary, almost affectionate, in his dealings with me. Even took me out for dinner often if we were working late.

One summer day, he invited me on his boat. It would be a weekend trip to Michigan. I was excited.

By the end of that trip, we were lovers. We kept our relationship very quiet but it was becoming intense.

A few months went by and Alice was due to return soon.

I was on the telephone making an appointment for him for the following Thursday.

He interrupted me. "Cancel that. We are going to Las Vegas on Thursday to get married." That was his proposal. I could hardly speak to end the phone call.

After Alice came back, I left the firm. We were looking for a house in the city. The apartment was too small and he also told me it would be nice if we had a family, although he felt it was unlikely since he had been married years before and no pregnancy had resulted.

We found a nice home in the city and started to furnish it. No surprise, he chose almost everything. I really did not mind since a girl from a farm did not have very sophisticated taste.

Besides, I was thrilled to be married and happy with this extraordinary man.

On his 50th birthday, I gave him his greatest gift. I was three months pregnant. He was out of his mind with joy. He took over the pregnancy. I knew he was controlling but sometimes, I wondered which one of us was having the baby. He read every book on pre-natal care, went to every doctor visit, was present for every test, weighed me every day, monitored my vitamins. He controlled everything like I was his most important stock client.

Alexander was a beautiful and healthy baby. We both were so happy. I was nursing but he insisted I have a nurse and a housekeeper. He, of course, interviewed both. After a week, I let the nurse go. I convinced him if you were nursing, she had very little to do.

Alexander flourished. He was treated like the Second Coming. He grew up to be a wonderful young man. His father took him everywhere he went, even sometimes to the office.

Friends were not very welcome in our home. If someone dropped in, he was not hospitable. It was him, me and of course this beloved son. It was like he wanted us all to himself.

There were times when he was wonderful. Especially if we were traveling. He was the man of my dreams if we were in an interesting place in the world.

Otherwise, he just wanted to be at home. He called it his "island."

He wouldn't go out for dinner, but if I said, "Let's go to Paris," he was ready to pack his suitcase. Of course, Alexander had a RN to stay with him. Besides the housekeeper.

I got the idea of opening a travel agency. Amazingly, he approved. He loved travel. He would come and help me with it.

It really helped me to get over feeling

isolated. After Alexander was in school, I had little to do.

Julius became ill with cancer. It was serious but after a few treatments, he just ignored it. His main reaction was anger. He continued working every day but became more and more difficult at home.

The cancer came back with a vengeance. The anger was now directly targeted towards me; His most frequent criticism was that I had to "grow up." It was never explained.

There were many times I even thought of leaving him but "Minnesota Nice" people can't do that. I had to stay. And Alex was a teenager and very traumatized by his father's illness. He never was anything but loving toward him. I had to consider him too.

I always heard people died peacefully. Not Julius. He was yelling, "NO! NO!" for the last minutes he was alive. Then, he just slipped away. I hope he is at rest.

Julius is my past now. I have to start all over. I just don't know where to start except to do his funeral arrangements. I'll think about my life later. Maybe I'll learn how to "grow up."

Chapter Two

The pretty redhead, forty year old widow, Megan and her lovely, younger, blonde sister, June, are seated at the Funeral Director's desk. June has come in from New York to help with the funeral.

The large, florid faced man is asking questions and filling out forms.

His assistant, Irving, stands behind him. Both are dressed impeccably and are wearing sympathetic faces befitting the somber occasion.

All four walk down a hall.

A door opens from the lit hall and a hand reaches for a light switch, revealing a huge room filled with coffins. They usher in the women.

The two women gasp at the sight.

The Funeral Director speaks –

"Dear ladies, I know what a shock it is to come in here. We want to make it as easy as we can for you. And, of course do the right thing for Julius. This is his final curtain call and we are going to make it perfect for him."

Megan agrees. "Yes, we want it nice, don't we, June?"

June nods. "Julius always liked the best."

The ghost of Julius, the deceased husband, walks into the coffin room. He is wearing a white dinner jacket and smoking a cigar.

The funeral director speaks to his assistant.

"Irving, move a couple of these boxes out of the way. I want to show the ladies

Mrs.Updike's husband's casket. She was so happy with it. It is just the perfect chariot for Julius' journey to Eternity."

"Oh, yes. The beautiful copper one."

"You know the Updikes of course. They live on the Gold Coast. Wonderful people and also such a terrible loss."

"This one is so perfect. Look at the mattress. Three inches. It will be so comfortable for your dear Julius."

He grabs June's hand to have her feel it. She pulls her hand back in horror.

"And the color of the satin. Pale pink. So flattering to the complexion. We need all the help we can get at a time like this."

Megan looks worried. "What does something like this cost?"

"Oh it is quite reasonable when you take into consideration all that is included. The two limos, the opening of the grave and the WATERTIGHT liner. We fondly refer to this package as *The Emperor*. It's pure elegance."

Megan frowns."It looks expensive".

"Not really. The entire package is $30,000."

The ghost of Julius flacks his cigar ash on the carpet. "*What a crock. This guy's last job must have been as a used car salesman. I damn well am not going to spend that kind of money for this funeral. And, what are we doing here? I didn't die or anything.*"

Megan seems to hear a voice. She looks around and sees no one. "Did you hear a voice, June?"

June shakes her head.

Megan turns back to the Funeral Director.
"Look, I want to spend $8000. What can I buy for
$8000?"
The ghost of Julius throws his hands up in
disgust.
*You women do not know how to
negotiate. Never reveal your bottom line.*

The Funeral Director rolls his eyes at his
assistant.
"Well, we will be hard pressed to deliver your
Beloved Julius' funeral at that price. Please do
Not even mention watertight liners at that cost
Just don't even go there.

Megan is getting impatient. "I'd like to get this
over with."
"Irving, get Number 9 and wheel it over here."
"The silver one with the gray lining?"
"No, Irving,that is Number 8."
He turns to the women to explain.
"Number 9 has a much younger look."

Megan and June look at each other and
try not to laugh.
The ghost of Julius adds to the
conversation.
*People always say I look young for my
age.*
The women start to leave. The ghost tries
to block the door.

*Wait. What are we doing here? Go back
and cancel all this. I did not die.*

Chapter Three

The funeral service has ended. The widow, her sister and her teenage son, Alex, are walking toward a limousine for the funeral procession.

Alex whispers to his mother.

"Do you think I should apologize to everyone Dad insulted?"

"No, Alie. People only remember the good things. Besides, it would take too long."

"So, what should I say to everybody?"

June answers him, "Just say, "thank you for coming.""

As they are about to get into the limousine, Irving, the assistant funeral director pulls Megan aside.

"Yes?"

"This may be the wrong t-time to ask you, but are you-seeing anyone?"

Megan looks horrified and gets into the car. Behind Irving, the ghost of Julius appears. He flicks his cigar ash in Irving's general direction.

Gettatahere you PUNK. She's way out of your league.

Another figure appears behind the ghost of Julius.

Danny is a short, rotund "angel" wearing a wrinkled suit and a battered fedora. His job is to escort Julius to the other side He arrives flustered and out of breath.

.

Where have you been? I thought you

were right behind me and when I looked you were gone. I've got such a headache over this.

Who the hell are you?

I'm Danny. I'm your agent.

Agent?

Some of the people over here call themselves angels but this is my first job.

Since when do I need an agent?

We take you over to the other side. You don't live on earth anymore.

I'm not going anywhere with you. Now, scram!

I'm going to have to report this to The Committee. You are screwing up their statistics.

Danny takes his cell phone out of his pocket.

We got problems here. You told me this was an easy booking.

Chapter Four

Megan is pulling into a parking space outside her travel agency. It is located in a strip mall in the outskirts of Chicago. There are posters in the window advertising various travel destinations and airlines. Halfway in, the old Lincoln stalls. She restarts the car, parks it and walks inside the agency.

A bell rings when the front door is opened. There is a main front office with four desks, two on each side, and each with a computer. Racks of brochures line the side walls. Some are curled over and look messy.

Sally sits at the front desk
"You have clients waiting for you in your office. I gave them their tickets but they want to say hello."
"Oh, thanks, Sally."
Megan has a private office with a larger desk and a computer. There are bookcases on the wall behind her and two chairs for clients in front of the desk.
Megan enters her office. Two elderly ladies are seated. They stand to greet her.
"So nice to see you, Megan. We came in to pick up our tickets to Florida. You look wonderful."
The second elderly lady adds –
"So sorry to hear about your husband. What a terrible loss. How are you, dear?"
Megan starts to answer but the ladies continue to talk.
"You're a young, attractive woman. You'll

find someone. Take my advice. Look for someone younger this time. They last longer."

As they leave, one of the clients turns to Megan.

"Don't wait too long. Time marches on. A woman without a man is a terrible thing."

As the ladies turn and start to walk out, one of them asks.

"Are you seeing anyone yet?"

Megan tries not to look shocked when she answers.

"Not quite yet."

Megan sits down and starts opening the piles of mail on her desk.

Chapter Five

My husband Julius, as a stockbroker, didn't know the travel business. But that never stopped him from coming in here after the market closed and telling everybody what to do.They did not like him.

I don't know how many times I had to remind him. "There can be only one boss here." He never listened.

He had nothing but distain for my employees in the travel agency. He always referred to my staff as "the zoo."

I have to admit they were characters but it never bothered me because they got the work done. And they always helped each other if one of them was overwhelmed. I do admit they were "different."

First there is Catherine, who is staring at her computer. She is wearing jeans, a sweater and John Lennon glasses.

Catherine is a 25 year old spinster in the making.She has clients among the wealthy Southside Irish of Chicago so she is a valuable employee. But she booked a sick man who was going to the Mayo Clinic in Rochester, Minnesota into Rochester, New York, so she has to be watched.

Catherine (looks up as though remembering)

"I was so happy when I got him on a nonstop flight."

The roar of a motorcycle is heard outside. Nick is seen through the glass front door taking off on his Harley. Annie walks into the office and takes her seat.

Annie used to teach kindergarten. She has had a series of boyfriends - motorcyclists – who kept.her up late. She doesn't ride one herself. I think she just likes the "Macho" attitude they have.

Sally always has something to say.

"A nice girl like you shouldn't be hanging around with scooter trash".

"He's not scooter trash. Nick is a member of the Hell's Angels. That's like royalty."

Sally picks up a telephone call.

Sally runs the show around here. We don't know much about her personal life except she's been divorced and is very involved with her sister's kids. She has a clientele of Russian immigrants. No one can handle them but her.

Sally is talking to one of them.

"Wait, wait, and listen to me. This is the cheapest fare. Did I get you a good deal to Fort Lauderdale last year? Do I take care of you? Listen! And what about your sister? Did I get her a cabin on the cruise ship really cheap?"

Linda is arriving at the office. She stumbles and almost falls. Linda is involved in a messy divorce and sometimes has an over medication problem. She is always complaining about something.

"We've got to fix this carpet. It's dangerous."

Catherine answers.

"Megan already had it fixed."

Linda sits down at the third desk.

Harriet is sitting behind Sally filing her nails.

Harriet is married to Shelley. She is a compulsive talker and will continue a conversation with you even if you leave the room.

"Last night I made such a wonderful roast. Shelley doesn't make me cook. But I said to Shelley –"

Sally interrupts her.

"Please. I'm trying to concentrate"

So, that's the group. Believe or not, we actually do some business although it has been a little slow around here.

I am hoping bookings will pick up soon. I've been out a lot because Julius has been so sick. But, I'm back in the saddle again.

Chapter Six

The women lunch together in the back office at a large table. Deli sandwiches are being delivered by Mike. He barks the orders out.

"Who gets the BLT? The turkey on white? The turkey on wheat? Tuna? Here. Here's the invoice. You girls figure it out. I want to talk to Megan."

Megan is on the telephone with a client. Mike leans on the doorway.

"Excuse me, can you hold on a minute?"

Megan puts her call on hold and looks up at Mike. He smoothes his hair and forces a smile.

"Hello, Mike. What can I do for you?"

"I just wanted to tell you how sorry I am about the passing of your husband."

"That's sweet of you."

"I just wanted to tell you if there's anything I can do —"

"Thank you Mike. I'm doing just fine."

Mike musters up courage and comes to the point —

"The Meatpackers Union is having their annual ball Saturday night. It costs $40.00 a couple. We could split it."

Megan is speechless. Mike decides to sweeten the offer.

"I'll pay for gas and parking."

"Thanks, Mike. I'm not ready. Look, I'm sorry, but I'm on the phone."

Megan finishes her call and goes to the lunchroom. The women are hungrily eating their sandwiches and talking.

The ghost of Julius and Danny are seated at the table.

Megan is obviously annoyed about something.

"Did you hear what those women said this morning? Am I seeing anyone yet? It's been a month."

Annie nods.

"People think you are nothing if you don't have a man."

Catherine joins in, "Speaking of men, how is the divorce going, Linda?"

"Slow. Very slow. He's back living with "the child," you know."

Sally asks. "What child?"

"That bimbo he's shacked up with. She's 20. He bought her a sable coat and then, I hear he beat her up. He does that, you know."

Megan shakes her head sympathetically.

"A man is the last thing I have on my mind. You know how difficult Julius could be. Sometimes I feel he's still around. And I hate to say this because you will think I am crazy, but there are times I can hear him talking to me."

Sally looks at Megan.

"That is crazy. Julius was a good guy. A little opinionated but —"

The ghost of Julius is defensive at Sally's remark.

Being right is not opinionated!

Catherine adds her experience.

"My mother stayed in the house after she died. I'd come home at night and I could hear her rattling pots in the kitchen. She gave me recipes in my sleep."

The women react with astonishment at that remark.

Megan is interested in what she has to say.

"You're kidding me! How long did she stay around?"

"For a while. I talked to a psychic about it. He said that some spirits just don't want to leave."

Sally is obviously uncomfortable talking about the departed.

"This is a crazy conversation. Dead is dead."

"Then, where did I get those recipes? You know I can't cook."

Megan ponders that thought.

The ghost of Julius adds to the conversation.

Nobody's dead around here. I never felt better in my life.

Sally wants to end the discussion.

"That's what I like about being involved with my sister's kids. No husbands, laundry, homework or chickenpox."

Lunch is over. The women are clearing off the table.

Sally looks at Megan.

"What are you going to do with all that freedom?"

Megan hesitates and then blurts out.

"I want to get my eyes done. I feel old and worn out."

The ghost of Julius walks out of the room. He is annoyed.

He turns to Danny who is following him.

And that, without a doubt, is the stupidest

idea she ever had.

Catherine gets up from the table and cleans off her area.

"I am glad to get home to my books and my cat. By the way; I'd like you all to remember Blackie in your prayers."

Linda looks very skeptical at the idea.

"You want us to pray for a cat?"

"My vet says he has a tumor. I hope it's benign."

Megan is going back to work. She turns to Catherine.

"We'll all keep Blackie in our good thoughts."

Chapter Seven

There is a conference room which seems to be floating in the sky. It is blinding, brilliant white.

A group of shadowy white figures are sitting around a long table covered with a white tablecloth.

Danny is sitting at the far end of the table.

A man with a long white beard, who is also clothed in white, is at the head of the table.

He opens the meeting and seems to be the Chairman.

"First on the agenda is Danny. We've had a good week. All except you, Danny. Where is Julius?"

"This is the toughest booking of my career, Chief."

"Have you told him that he will be happier with us here? That we will teach him how to do it over next time he in the earth plane?"

Danny tries to explain.

"You can't tell Julius anything. This guy will not accept his life is over. He thinks he can get back into it and do things over now. He won't even listen to me. He is very stubborn. I don't know why I got such a difficult booking for my first assignment."

The Chairman continues -

"You told us that after being a theatrical agent, anything would be easy. Do you want another assignment?"

"No, no. I think I can convince him but I need some time. I never give up. You have no idea of the difficult bookings I have done. This is

a slightly different business being an angel."
The Chairman has the last word.
"We'll give you some time. But, you've got a clock on you, Danny. Get it done."

Chapter Eight

Megan lives in a yellow brick, Georgian house, on a small lot in Chicago. She has parked her car in the driveway and is walking into the front door with groceries.

She puts the groceries away and goes upstairs to find her son, Alex.

Alex occupies a standard teenage room. Posters. Unmade bed. Clothes on the floor. Rock music is blasting.

She knocks loudly on the door. "Alex, could I come in for a minute?"

Alex turns off the music and opens the door.

"Look, I want to apologize for what I said about your writing the household checks from now on."

"I thought it would help you if I did what Dad did. I know you miss him."

"I do, Alie. But, there's plenty of time for you to have those responsibilities."

"I wouldn't mind doing it."

"And I don't want you to think you have to stay home with me. I want you to go out and have fun."

"I don't want you to be alone, Mom."

Alex comes over and gives her a hug.

"Please, Alie. I want you to be a kid. Just be a kid. That would help me the most."

Megan was pleased that Alex went out with his friends that evening.

It also gave her some time to have a talk on the telephone with her sister, June.

The ghost of Julius and Danny are listening to the conversation.

"June, I keep telling you, Julius is still around. He has something to say to me about everything. Just like he always did. I hope I am not going nuts."

Megan pauses as she listens to her sister.

"All right, I'll try to ignore it."

Danny begins lecturing the ghost of Julius.

See, you are not supposed to be here. It's against the rules.

Obviously, the ghost of Julius does not welcome Danny being around all the time.

How did you get to be assigned to me anyway? I've avoided sleazeballs like you all my life.

Maybe so you'll learn there are no sleazeballs. We are all the same.

Chapter Nine

The ghost of Julius is entering a large office building. He is wearing a suit and tie and carrying a briefcase. Danny runs in behind him.

Where are you going?

To my office, stupid. I've been out sick. God knows what they've done with my clients.

I wouldn't advise it, Julius.

Who asked you for advice?

They are now ascending in a crowded elevator.

Danny is concerned.

You're not going to like what you find. Trust me.

They get off the elevator and the ghost of Julius greets the receptionist at the front desk of his office.

Good morning, Helen.

The receptionist does not hear him.

They walk through the office. The ghost of Julius greets several people on the way. No one responds. He pauses at the door of his office. The nameplate is not his. John, a young broker is sitting at his desk talking on the telephone.

"OK, George, I'll sell the T-bills and buy Microsoft for you today."

The ghost of Julius steps up to the desk and wags his finger in John's face. John does not flinch.

Hey, that's my client you're talking to! Don't you dare sell his T-bills. You're churning him.

Danny calls out from the doorway.

He can't hear you, Julius. Let's go.

John hangs up the phone and calls out to Alice, now his assistant. He picks up a small box from the floor.

"Alice, when are you going to get this junk out of my office?"

Alice enters the room.

"I'll send it out to Julius' wife later today."

"Not that she needs any more reminders of that pompous ass. What was his problem, anyway?"

"He was an okay guy, John. He sure loved his kid."

"His kid belongs to an elite club. Julius was a professional stockbroker but an amateur human being."

Alice's phone is ringing. She hurries out to answer it. John idly rummages through the box, takes out a gold pen, looks at it, shrugs and puts it in his desk drawer.

Look at that, Danny. The guy is a thief!

See? I told you not to come here.

A dejected ghost of Julius slowly walks out of the office. He and Danny get into the elevator.

You don't know who your friends are until you're half dead.

Danny sadly answers.

You're completely dead.

They walk out of the elevator.

I'm coming back. See? And you're going to help me.

Danny looks upward toward heaven.

Oy! Why me?

Chapter Ten

A Policeman has his siren on behind Megan's big Lincoln. She doesn't stop. The siren continues. She looks at her rear view mirror, turns around, and motions to the policeman, as if to say –"ME?" She finally stops and pulls over.

The policeman walks to her car.

"You just made an illegal left turn. Didn't you see that sign?"

"No, I'm sorry officer, I didn't."

"Your license plates expired four months ago. And your city sticker expired two months ago."

"Oh."

"I'm going to have to give you three tickets."

"My husband died. He always took care of the cars."

"I'm sorry to hear about your husband but you're going to have to get it together, lady."

"Okay. I will."

He is writing tickets as he talks.

"And this is none of my business, but the sticker on your car says you haven't changed the oil in 10,000 miles. Change it."

"OK. I will."

The ghost of Julius is sitting with Danny in the back seat of the car as she drives home.

Do you know what three tickets are going to cost me?

Chapter Eleven

The ghost of Julius is trying to make a telephone call. He is pushing the numbers and nothing is happening. Danny is reading the paper and looks up.

Who do you think you're calling?
My lawyer, Sidney. I'm going to have him draw up a living will. I don't want that burden on Megan in case anything happens to me. Hello. Hello.
It's too late for that.

The ghost of Julius is trying to dial again.
Hello. Hello. Damn! I have to talk to Megan about replacing this phone.
They can't hear you, Julius. When are you going to realize you don't live on the earth anymore?

Julius is furious.
And when are you going to stop bugging me and get lost? I have business to take care of.

Chapter Twelve

The bride and groom are dancing on a crowded dance floor. Megan is all dressed up and sitting alone at a table for ten. Everyone else is dancing.

The next day, Megan is rollerblading with her girlfriend, Arlene.

"I'm not a bit surprised. Married women do not want us around. We're a threat. It's a couple's world."

Megan is incredulous.

"Come on. These women know I'm not interested in their husbands. Julius and I have known these people for years."

Arlene explains.

"Trust me. Look, here's the formula. If you want to see them, entertain. If you invite them twice, they will feel obligated to invite you once. Then someone might ask you to dance next time."

Arlene hesitates and then says.

"By the way, I am having a dinner party. I know you'll understand. My table seats ten and if I invite you I'll waste an empty chair. I have to ask the Andersons. I owe them an invitation. You know how it is."

"That's terrible. I always included you. You're single."

Arlene is embarrassed. Megan is right.

"It's just this one time. I thought you'd understand."

The ghost of Julius and Danny are also on rollerblades trying to keep up with the women.

Hey! Wait up. You're going too fast.

The women quickly leave them behind.

The ghost of Julius calls out after them.

      I always told you Arlene was a waste of time.

      Danny is struggling not to fall off the rollerblades.

      This is very dangerous. I'm going to end up in a hospital with this booking.

Chapter Thirteen

Megan is conferring with a salesman at a garden center.

"Could give me some advice? These Impatiens say shade and the Geraniums say sun. Can I plant them together?"

The ghost of Julius is listening.

Put those red geraniums back. We had red last year. We'll have pink this year.

Megan is seen loading the trunk of her car with pink geraniums.

The ghost of Julius and Danny get in the back seat and ride home with Megan.

She has an appointment with her friend, Johnny, who is an interior decorator.

They are in the living room which has dark walls and heavy red velvet drapes. Johnny has paint chips and he is holding them up to the wall.

"I want everything light, Johnny, a big change. And I always hated these drapes. And, that chair needs reupholstering."

The ghost of Julius disagrees with everything.

That color is too light. And what's wrong with the drapes? I like my chair just as it is. It does not need reupholstering.

Danny is weary after the busy day.

Julius, leave her alone. It is not your house anymore. Or your garden. You are dead.

The ghost of Julius is furious.

Get out of my house, you creep. Just go

back to whatever Committee you report to and tell them I am not dead and you got fired.

Chapter Fourteen

The women are opening cartons of Thai food. There is a roar of a motorcycle outside.

Annie gets off a Harley chopper from behind a leather-jacketed man. He leans over and kisses her. Then he whacks her on the behind.

"Sorry I'm late. I was detained against my will."

Sally is annoyed.

"Until lunchtime?"

"I'll make it up, Megan. I'll stay late."

Megan continues the conversation that Annie interrupted.

"Anyway, as I was saying, I was thinking about taking a cruise. We just got a very reasonable offer to the Caribbean. What do you think?"

Catherine agrees.

"I think you should do it. Just do it. You haven't been anywhere for a long time."

"I'm going to do it."

The ghost of Julius and Danny has arrived in the office to hear the last of the conversation.

Good idea. I could use a vacation.

Danny is very annoyed.

This is not part of my contract. I hate water.

Who invited you?

Chapter Fifteen

A sunburned Megan is unpacking her suitcase in her bedroom and putting things away. She is talking to her sister June on the phone.

"I had a horrible time. The ship was full of widows. They sat us together. And every single one of us had sequin dresses."

She takes a sequin dress out of the suitcase and hangs it in the closet.

"Let me paint the picture for you. There were ten widows at my table. And there were another ten at three other tables. All women gowned in sequin dresses."

I introduced myself.

"This is my first trip alone. It's an experience."

One of the women answers.

"You'll get used to it. I felt that way when Harry first passed on."

The widow dismissed Megan with that remark. The women go on with their conversation which all runs together.

"I want to tell you girls about the darling camel seat I got in St. Thomas today."

"What did you pay for it?"

"It took me an hour of bargaining but I got him down to $19.00."

"I bought one right on the pier in San Juan yesterday for $15.00."

"When I was in Tangiers, on another ship, I saw them for $10.00."

They all start studying the menu.

"So what are we going to have for dessert? I think I'll order all of them."

"The sea air is shrinking all my clothes."

"I always wear my thin clothes first. Are we playing bridge tonight?"

"We need our strength for jewelry at H. Stern in Caracas tomorrow."

"I'm going up to the nightclub and heckle that terrible magician. He's very attractive."

"I tried to get into the conversation, June." They were all interrupting each other.

"Is there dancing after the show?"

One of the ladies answered me.

"Don't be delusional. The captain is a drunk. The cruise staff is gay. And the officers won't dance with you unless you are under 30."

Another widow chimed in.

"You want to dance? Go back to Chicago. Find yourself a nice guy and bring him with you next time. You'll learn."

I decided to just go back to my cabin

.

The next day, I took a book I was reading and went up on deck. A woman approached me.

"Is anyone sitting here?"

"No, please sit down."

The woman settles down with her things and starts applying sun block.

Then, she asked me.

"Are you traveling alone?"

"Yes. I'm a new widow. I hate it."

"I remember those days myself. It's hard to start a whole new life. But, let me give you a little advice. Start."

"I don't even know how to start."

The ghost of Julius is in his bathing suit sunning himself on a deck chair. He is wearing a Panama hat and sunglasses.

You could start by growing up, you know.

Danny is sitting on a deck chair next to the ghost of Julius in his wrinkled suit. He is wearing sunglasses and his hat is pulled down over his eyes. He is fanning himself as his cell phone is ringing.

Where am I? On a stinking ship in the middle of an ocean for Chrissakes!
Humidity always killed me.

Who was that?
It's the Committee Chairman. You're still showing absent on his computer printout and he is hopping mad.
Tell him to scratch me off his list. They are not taking me alive.

"So, June, that's the story. I'm never going on a cruise alone again. You are going to have to get over your seasickness so you can go with me."

"I'll speak to my doctor to see if there is anything new on the market. I'd love to go with you."

Chapter Sixteen

Alex is having breakfast. Megan has a thick sheaf of papers and she is intently filling them out.

"What are all those papers, Mom?"

"It's an application the Veterans Administration sent me."

"What are you applying for?"

"I have no idea."

"Then why are you doing all that work?"

"Your Dad was in their Navy. You never know. We might be entitled to something."

She kisses Alex –

"Gotta run. I'm late. See you at dinner."

Sally meets her at the door.

"Annie is in your office. She's upset. The church canceled the Israel tour."

Annie is sitting on a chair in front of Megan's desk and is sobbing.

"Maybe we can offer them another destination. A lot of international trips are being canceled."

"I already tried that. The priest said they were not going anywhere. 40 people, Megan. I was counting on this commission."

"I know. So was I. It is a big loss in revenue for you and the agency."

Annie is still sniffling.

"Maybe I should get out of travel and go back to teaching kindergarten."

Megan is sympathetic. "This business is getting tougher and tougher every day."

Chapter Seventeen

A sign on the front door reads, "St. Jude's Widows Support Group." There is a greeter to meet the widows.

The ghost of Julius and Danny follow Megan in.

What the hell is she doing here?

Maybe she just wants to find some nice widows to hang out with. She's probably lonely.

How can she be lonely? I'm with her all the time. I talk to her. She listens.

Danny hesitates before he answers.

She thinks she is imagining it. I have to talk to the Committee about this. She should not be hearing a dead man. I don't understand it. This is not what is supposed to be happening.

This just goes to prove you are a failure. You know nothing about anything. She needs me and I am not dead.

The greeter continues to talk to Megan.

"It's nice to meet you, Megan. How long have you been a widow?"

"It's been a little while now."

"Oh, I'm sorry you didn't come sooner. Please come in."

About twelve older women are sitting in chairs with desk arms. Some are crying. The speaker is at the podium.

"Good evening ladies. Are you all set for our program? Now, each of you has a sample check in front of you. Have you got it? Does everyone have a pen? Good. Now let's start from the top. Fill in the date. Now go down to where it says "Pay to the order of." That's where you put in the person or business you are paying. After that you write in the amount in figures."

The woman sitting next to Megan fills out her check and compares it with Megan's to see if it is correct.

"Now here's the tricky part .Look at the next line. It ends in "dollars.""

Megan is trying to slip out quietly. The greeter stops her.

"Are you leaving?"

"Yes, I have to go. I have an early appointment tomorrow."

"Oh, I'm so sorry. You'll be missing "The Mystery of the Bank Statement." It's just fascinating."

"Perhaps another time".

The ghost of Julius is pulling on his camel hair coat.

What a waste of time. I always handle the bank statements anyway.

Chapter Eighteen

Megan is stretching out on a mat next to two women at her health club. She is listening to their conversation.

"It cost Sylvia $40,000.00 but I'll tell you, her own mother wouldn't recognize her. She had EVERYTHING done – face – boobs – tummy tuck and a fanny lift."

"I hear she is dating a 38 year architect. She's 60 if she is a day."

Megan is thinking. "It sure would be nice to have that kind of extra money."

The ghost of Julius is standing nearby in his designer sweats.

Why do you waste your time listening to those silly broads?

Megan gets off the mat and starts running on the treadmill. The ghost of Julius gets on the treadmill next to her.

OK. I'm going to give you a break. Call Alice at the brokerage house and put in a buy order for 500 shares of IBM at 118. As soon as it hits, tell her to put in a sell order at 130. Our roof needs replacing and the car needs work. You'll pick up enough money to fix them.

Megan wonders, "Am I going crazy? Can I be hearing this?"

The ghost of Julius continues. *Just do what I tell you for a change. But don't be greedy. Sell at 130.*

Back at the agency, Megan is telling the girls what she heard.

"I think I'm going to do it."

Sally pulls out the newspaper. "Let's look it up."

They all examine the stock prices in the Chicago Tribune

"This is crazy, Megan. IBM is selling at 150. Your broker is going to laugh at you."

Annie is excited. "I think she should do it."

"I'm going to call Alice right now."

Megan leaves the lunchroom to call Alice.

Harriet puts her opinion out.

"Maybe we should check with Shelley. He knows about —"

Catherine interrupts.

"If I can get recipes, why can't she get a stock tip?"

Linda is sarcastic.

"Maybe we'd do more business around here doing séances."

Megan returns to the lunchroom.

"The order is in."

Sally wants to know.

"Did she think you were crazy?"

"Alice said if anyone could get a message out from the grave it would be Julius."

The ghost of Julius is standing outside the doorway and has been overseeing the transaction. Danny is with him.

Grave? What grave? I've got a good thirty years left in me.

Not on this side you don't.

I've made mistakes. I have to do some things over.

Danny attempts to explain. *"You don't understand. You can't change the past. It's over.*

The women are filing out of the lunchroom to go back to work

Sally remembers to give Megan a message.
"By the way, Megan, the Green couple called. I think they are going to buy that World Cruise. They are coming in today to discuss it."

Later, Megan is walking an elegantly dressed couple to the door.
"Send us postcards. You'll have wonderful time seeing the world. It's going to be so exciting."

The couple leaves. Megan takes a key out of her pocket and quickly locks the door to the agency. She picks up the phone on Sally's desk and calls the local police. Most of them are clients of the agency.

"This is Megan at the travel agency. Could you send someone over? We have $95,000 in cash to take to the bank."
The police are there in five minutes.

Annie and Linda walk out of the agency and get in Linda's car. They follow the police car, sirens blasting. When they get to the bank, Annie gets out and goes into the bank while Eric, the policeman, waits outside. Annie comes out of the bank.
"Thanks for the escort. I don't think I've seen you before. Are you new on the force?
"Yes. Just got out of the Academy. I'm Eric."

"Well, hello Eric. I'm Annie. Nice to meet you."

Linda and Annie are riding back in the car to the agency.

"That new cop is kinda cute. Linda, I never saw so much money at one time. All in cash. They had three tellers counting it. And I can't pay my Visa bill."

"How come?"

Annie is crying.

"I got a $500.00 cash advance on my Visa card. I figured the commission on the church tour would cover it."

"What for?"

"Don't say anything but I had to bail Nick out of jail. One of his old girlfriends said he threw her down the stairs. She has a concussion."

"Annie, you've only known that guy a couple of months."

"I believe Nick. I couldn't let an innocent man sit in jail."

"Annie?"

"What?"

"Be careful."

"Don't worry I always wear a helmet when I ride with him on his motorcycle".

"That's not what worries me."

Chapter Nineteen

Jeffrey, the accountant, walks in to Megan's office with spreadsheets and sits down.

"So, how bad do things look?"

"The quarter is not good. I don't see any invoices here for Acme Press. What happened to them?"

Megan explains. "They have a moratorium on salesman travel right now."

"How's the fall shaping up?"

"We've had some cancellations. But we're hoping things will get better. I sold a World Cruise this week."

"You're going to have to put some money in here again to keep the agency going."

The ghost of Julius is annoyed.

If you had built an organization like I told you – you wouldn't be in this mess.

Megan is depressed. This is not good news. She is looking forward to a quiet weekend to absorb it.

It is Sunday morning at home. Megan is reading the *Chicago Tribune* in her chair. Danny is standing, reading the *Hollywood Reporter.* The ghost of Julius is reading *the New York Times* on the couch. Alex is sitting on the other side of the couch, studying.

"Listen to this, Mom. Thoreau wrote it. It's from Walden. *If one advances confidently in the direction of his dreams, and endeavors to live the life he has imagined, he will meet with a success unexpected in common hours.*

"Mom, are you listening?"

"Yes, I'm listening, Alex. That's really beautiful."

"Dad said he was paying big numbers for my education and I wouldn't make a dime studying philosophy."

The ghost of Julius looks up from his paper.

Listen, son, I'm changing. I want whatever makes you happy.

"Alex looks thoughtful.

"I want to study things that will benefit my whole life. I'll think about money later."

"Your Dad was always saving for retirement. It was his way of loving us."

Alex picks up his books and makes a comment as he walks out of the room.

"He never got to retire. I'm not going to live like that."

The ghost of Julius turns to Danny.

What a wonderful kid. That's why I have to come back. I can't afford to retire.

Chapter Twenty

Megan is arriving at the office when Sally says, "You've got a call on line two. I think it's your broker."

She races to the phone.

"Oh, my God, Alice. It really happened? I can't believe it. No, I don't want to buy anything else. No, he didn't give me any more messages. Just send me a check."

Megan runs out to tell Sally.

"Sally. It happened just like he said. I made almost $5000."

At lunch, everyone is very excited about Megan's good fortune.

Catherine is thrilled.

"See, Sally. I told you. You can get messages. Just like I told you."

"Don't lecture me, Catherine. Today I'm a believer. Let me know if you get any more stock tips."

Annie adds, "Me too. I wish I had some money to invest."

Harriet says, "I told Shelley about it. I told him, "Shelley, let's take a chance, Shelley. Let's do it."

Linda is smug. "I don't need investments. My lawyers just found bank accounts in Switzerland and in Cayman. That bastard was hiding a lot of money. When this divorce is over, I will be rich."

Catherine is excited for Megan.

"So what are you going to do with the

money, Megan?"

"I am calling the plastic surgeon. I'm going to have my eyes lifted. This windfall is found money. And it is going to give me a whole new outlook on life. I think I can get an appointment in a week."

The ghost of Julius is furious.

Found money? Found money? Who do you think found it? The roof and the car need fixing.

Danny has arrived in the office. The ghost of Julius is surprised to see him.

I thought you left.

I'm in and out. There's no money on the other side you know.

No money? How do people live?

They don't live. They're dead.

I don't get it.

Danny gives him a little lecture.

You'll learn that wealth is in your mind and your heart. And being grateful for what you have. Not in getting things.

How do you learn that?

Danny explains.

Study. Then you get a new life on earth and can practice.

I need a new life now. Today.

Danny tries to continue. *Are you kidding me? With your record, you'll be learning lessons for a hundred years before they let you come back.*

Chapter Twenty-One

Megan is in the front hall in her bathrobe. Alex has his coat on and is swinging his book bag over his shoulder. He is on his way to classes.

"What are they going to do to you in the hospital?"

"A little procedure. A nothing. I'm taking the bus downtown today."

"Should I worry?"

"Of course not. For some stupid reason, I have to spend the night."

"Call me when you are through and I'll come down and pick you up."

Megan is getting off an elevator on the eighth floor. She hands some papers to the receptionist.

Megan is in the X-RAY department having a chest X-RAY.

A technician is taking blood samples.

Megan is on a table having an EKG.

"Are you sure my doctor ordered all these tests? You know I'm not having brain surgery."

The ghost of Julius and Danny are sitting in the waiting room. The ghost of Julius is reading *The Wall Street Journal.* Danny is nervously pacing

Let's get out of here. I hate hospitals. I feel faint.

Megan is now in a hospital gown and sitting up in bed. Arlene is pouring martinis into glasses and arranging some snacks on the bed tray.

"They are making such a fuss here. So many tests".

An Oriental doctor comes in with a clipboard.

"I have a few questions for you."

"You know, I have company right now. Check with all those people on the eighth floor. They know everything about me."

The Resident sits down anyway.

"When did you first notice your condition?"

Arlene is clicking glasses with Megan "Well, here's looking at the new you!"

The next morning, Megan is talking to Sally on the telephone.

"I didn't sleep a wink with the racket they make around here and at these prices, they don't even include breakfast."

An orderly is arriving with a stretcher.

Megan is not through talking to Sally.

"The Olson's are leaving for Paris tonight. I forgot to get them seats on Air France. As far forward as possible."

The orderly has her arm. "We have to go now. They want you now."

"Can you wait a minute? And order Mrs. Olson a seafood platter."

"I'll help you on the stretcher."

"You don't understand. This is business."

She is on the stretcher now.

"And Mr. Olson wants a vegetarian meal."

The orderly takes the phone away from Megan, hangs it up and wheels her out.

A few hours later, Megan is in bed in her hospital room after the eyelift. She has icepacks on her eyes. A nurse is taking her pulse.

"Your doctor wants you to go to the bathroom. I'll help you"

"I can go by myself."

She nearly falls. The nurse supports her and they slowly walk to the bathroom. She accidentally looks at herself in the mirror.

"OH MY GOD. IS THAT ME? WHAT DID HE DO TO ME?"

Her eyes are almost swollen shut. She has black stitches above and below her eyes.

"WHY DIDN'T ANYBODY TELL ME THIS WAS AN OPERATION?"

Her doctor comes in.

"Megan, everything went fine. You can go home this afternoon."

Chapter Twenty-Two

Alex is waiting for his mother at the hospital after the surgery. A nurse is delivering Megan to the car in a wheelchair. She gets out and throws her overnight bag into the back seat.

"You look really bad, Mom."

She doesn't answer.

When she gets home, Megan is in the den looking at a hand mirror she has propped on the end table. She is applying ice packs to her eyes and talking on the telephone to her attorney, Sidney.

"Sidney, I think we have a lawsuit here. Yes, I signed papers. A lot of papers. I'm very busy. I had no time to read them."

She pauses to listen to his answer.

"Sidney, you are not being supportive. Thanks for nothing."

She hangs up on Sidney and dials Sally at home.

"The way I look I don't think I will be back to work for a year."

The ghost of Julius is sitting on the couch. He gets up and turns on the TV.

He is in his white dinner jacket and has a martini in his hand.

Just look what you've done to yourself!
And the roof is still leaking. The car needs work.

Today Megan is in no mood to ignore the voice she hears.She yells at him.

"You can't stay here anymore, Julius."

Megan walks out of the room and returns with more ice.

If it wasn't for me –

He is slowly lighting his cigar. He puffs, and then studies the ash.

You'd be working in a 5 and 10 cent store in Minneapolis.

Danny walks into the room, fanning himself.

Oh no! You again! You're haunting me.

Do you have to smoke that stinky cigar in the house?

This is a Cuban cigar, moron. You have a peasant nose.

Danny's cell phone is ringing.

OK. OK. I'll come in.

Can you do me a favor? Have someone get me a Pastrami on rye from the Carnegie Deli in Manhattan. You've got to have a thousand angels in that territory.

What was that all about?

They're threatening to put me back in the Production Department. All because of you.

The movies?

No, babies. The crying drove me crazy. I could lose my job over you.

Good. Get out of here and don't come back.

You'll get me or somebody else.

Danny, I know about these things. These people you are dealing with are not business people. They need a good HR department. You'll never make it as an angel.

*Why don't you round up all your old
clients. They are probably all dead.*
Open a Comedy Club on the other side.
*They could use a few laughs. They might
go for it. What do you think?*
Danny is thinking.
*I would love that. But they won't even talk
to me about it until this job is finished.*

After a week, Megan is feeling much
better but she still can't show her face with
stitches in the office. She has to wear dark
glasses if she goes out. She is so bored.

Alex is in the upstairs study doing his
homework when Megan walks in.
"Alex, I've been thinking. Why don't we
sell this house and get a condo downtown?"
"Would we live near the lake?"
"Yes. We could live on Lake Shore Drive."
"That would be great. I wouldn't have to
cut the grass anymore."
Megan is driving Alex to school.
"You know if I sold the travel agency, we
could move to California."
"Boy, it sure would be great to get out of
the snow in the winter."
"And you could transfer to *USC*."
"That would be cool."
Alex is helping Megan bring in some
groceries.
"You know with your good grades, I bet
you could get into *Oxford*."
"England?"
""Yes. We could try it for a year. I could
sell the agency. There's nothing keeping us in

Chicago."

"We could visit Liverpool where the Beatles came from."

Megan and Alex are having dinner.

"It's so flat here in Chicago. Everywhere you go. Just flat."

"It's the Midwest."

"I was thinking how nice it would be to live in the mountains. Like Boulder, Colorado. There's a wonderful university there."

"You are driving me crazy, Mom."

What do you mean?

"Every day you want to move to a different place"

"I need a change in my life."

Alex starts clearing the table.

"When the moving van pulls up to the front door, let me know where we're going and I'll go with you."

The ghost of Julius is reading his paper at the table. He looks up over his half glasses. Danny is sitting next to him.

We're not moving anywhere. We are staying right here. We have too many memories here.

Danny sighs.

How many times do I have to say you don't live here anymore?

Chapter Twenty-Three

There is a client seated at Linda's desk with a very large, green parrot perched on his arm. She is talking to Delta Airlines.

"The Delta supervisor says you will have to buy him a seat if you want to take him to Florida on the plane."
Linda looks at him sternly.
"And he has to be in a cage."
"Even if he pays for his own seat?"
"Yes."
The client is thinking it over.
"Well, it is important that he goes to the funeral."
"What name should I put on the ticket?"
"Lucky. Lucky Shapiro. Just like my cousin."
Linda gets up to pull the tickets off the machine and complete the transaction.

In the meantime, the other women are talking to clients on the telephone.
Harriet is speaking.
"The room is $75.00. A nice hotel. Shelley and I stayed there."
Catherine is busy too.
"I can deliver your ticket. Tell me how to get to your house making all right hand turns."
Sally has problems with a client.
"What do you mean you missed the ship? No, they do not wait for people."
Harried continues her conversation about the hotel.
"When we went, I said to the woman, I

want to be up where I can see the river and she said for the river she gets $95.00. And I said to Shelley, no river's worth it to me."

Sally is impatient with her client.

"You will have to fly to the next stop in St. Maarten. No. They will not pay your airfare. You are supposed to be there when the ship sails."

The client and the parrot are leaving. The parrot breaks his silence and starts shrieking.

"HEY! YOU BITCH! JERK! JACKASS! WHORE!"

Everyone looks up in shock. Linda fills in with a bit of history.

"The passengers on that flight are in for a surprise. He told me the parrot was his cousin's "only child," so I decided to make the effort to get it approved. The bird was so quiet here."

Sally remarks.

"There are a million stories in this agency every day."

The ghost of Julius and Danny are watching the whole time.

"And you have the nerve to tell me I was wrong when I said this place is a zoo?

Chapter Twenty-Four

Megan makes a call to the agency to say she will be late today. She has an important stop to make.

She enters a local office of the Veterans Administration. There are several people waiting. She takes a number from the counter and sits down.

When her number is called, she sits at a desk with a woman counselor.

"What can I do for you?"

Megan nervously takes two letters out of her purse.

"Months ago, you made me fill out 60 pages of forms. Then, I got a letter from you saying I do not qualify for benefits because my income is over $170,000.00."

"I did not make you fill out forms. I did not write you the letter. It came from Washington."

Megan is persistent.

"Do I have to turn this over to my attorney? I just want to know where you found that money. Especially since I got a second letter saying I don't qualify for anything because I make over $4200.00. Where's the rest of the money?"

"Tell your attorney to contact Washington. Here is the address. They will tell you what you want to know".

Disappointed with the answer, she gets in her car and drives to the office. As usual, the car stalls as she pulls into the parking spot. She restarts it and pulls in.

Sally has a man with a Yarmulke on his

head at her desk. She is handing him his ticket.

He comes right to the point.

"So, by the way, do you cook?"

"Do you mean do I keep Kosher?"

"Yes."

"Not anymore."

"We have a nice singles group at our temple.Maybe you could come with me sometime. I'm a doctor you know."

She answers him abruptly.

"I'm pretty busy."

After the client leaves, Sally walks back to the lunchroom where the women are just finishing lunch.

Annie has heard the conversation.

"That guy was definitely hitting on you."

"I'm not interested. I'm through with slavery."

Linda agrees.

"There aren't any good men out there."

Harriet is finishing her sandwich.

"Shelley says lawyers are the worst. They just want to win the case."

Sally gets up to look for a file in the file cabinet.

"I can tell you doctors are cheap. And they think they are God. Even at home."

Linda adds another comment.

"Blue collar workers are too poor. And real estate or salesmen of any kind have no stable salary. Who wants to support these guys?"

Catherine is wiping off the table with a paper towel.

"The men who come in here from the corporations are all the same. Put them in a bottle. Shake them up. You pour out clones."

Annie is reapplying her lipstick.

"And workaholics. They have the money, but no time. And they are terrible in bed."

Linda sums it all up as she leaves the room.

"Like I said. There's nobody out there."

The ghost of Julius is leaning against the wall, nodding approvingly. Danny is with him.

That's because the good ones are all dead!

Danny is surprised.

Are you actually going to admit that?

Chapter Twenty-Five

Annie is late coming in. She has a black eye and her lip is swollen.

Harriet is upset.

"My God, Annie! What happened to you? Look at your face!"

"A stupid thing. I got up in the middle of the night and I ran into a door."

"That's terrible. You poor thing. You need to get some nightlights. Shelley says that most accidents happen at home."

Linda interrupts.

"Annie?"

"What?"

"I have an extra bedroom. Come and stay with me for a while."

Catherine chimes in.

"I bet you have nightlights."

"I do."

Annie is crying now.

"Give me some time to think about it."

Chapter Twenty-Six

It is crowded. A band is playing love songs. Megan is sitting at the bar with her girlfriend, Arlene.

"So this is the *Over 40 Singles Group*. I don't know, Arlene. These people look a lot older than 40 to me."

An elderly man is walking in. He is limping.

"Look at that guy coming in. He's ancient."

"Well, you said that you wanted to start getting out. Sometimes there's a younger crowd."

"Tonight doesn't seem to be the night."

The elderly man is tapping Megan on her shoulder.

"Would you like to dance?"

"You dance?"

"This is a nice slow number."

Megan is dancing with the elderly man. He puts both arms around her and starts fondling her behind. She pulls away from him.

"Look, you're going to have to excuse me. I have to go to the ladies room."

The ghost of Julius is laughing.

Well, that should make her appreciate what she already has.

Danny has something to say.

She doesn't have anyone, Julius. You are not here anymore.

Chapter Twenty-Seven

Thai food is being delivered today by Mr.Chuan, the owner of the restaurant. He collects the money and keeps looking toward the open door to Megan's office.

Mr. Chuan enters and bows politely.

"Sorry for trouble. You no more married lady?"

"No, Mr. Chuan, I'm not married anymore."

"Wife die. Long time now, Chuan no wife. You like married?"

Megan bows back.

"Maybe marry someday. Not ready now."

"Later I ask again."

Megan finally arrives in the lunchroom. She has had a busy morning.

Sally has to comment

"All our delivery men are in love with you."

"Other than our clients, they are the only men in my life."

Sally has a suggestion.

"Why don't you put a personal ad on-line?"

"I couldn't do that. I wouldn't know what to say."

"We'll all write it together. It'll be fun."

Linda has some experience with personal ads.

"Don't tell the truth about your age. Nobody will answer. Everyone lies. Make sure you say "financially secure." Of course they lie about that too. And don't mention the kid."

Annie adds, "As soon as I wrote I liked motorcycles, I got plenty of answers."

Harriet likes the idea.

"I'll ask Shelley what to say."

Catherine is excited about the idea.

"If I was in the market, I would do it".

So I made the decision to get out and find someone. I was finally ready. I had no idea of how many frogs there were out there and how hard it was going to be to locate one measly prince. I decided to call my attorney, Sidney, to see if he knew anyone. He fixed me up with one of his clients, Henry, who he said was a nice guy.

Megan enters an upscale restaurant. There are flowers on the tables and cozy red leather booths. She looks around for Henry, her lunch date. A heavy, bald man approaches Megan and they sit down in one of the booths.

"So you know Sidney. He's been our attorney for years."

She turns to the waitress.

"I think I'll have the tuna salad plate and a Diet Coke."

"That sounds good to me too. Make that two."

"Why don't you start by telling me a little about yourself?"

"Well, I was born in Iowa. No, wait a minute. I want to back up and tell you how my parents met. That's an interesting story."

Time lapse. The tuna salad is served.

"My mother always favored my brother and I think that probably contributed to my emotional problems."

The tuna salad has been eaten.

"I almost skipped telling you about my kindergarten teacher, Miss Curtis."

The Diet Coke is finished.

"Chicken pox was the worst, unless you want to count the tonsillectomy."

Megan speaks to the waitress.

"No, I'm fine. I've had enough Coke. And I don't want desert"

Henry continues.

"My first date stood me up. Why do women do things like that?"

Megan interrupts.

"I have to get back to the office. Say hello to Sidney. And thanks for the lunch."

"You're welcome. You're a wonderful conversationalist."

As Megan beats a rapid retreat, the ghost of Julius is sipping a martini and has been eavesdropping the whole time. Danny is with him. He calls after Megan.

How can you leave now? He's only up to age 16.

Then, he looks at Danny.

She's wasting her time. She'll never replace me.

What's so great about you?

It's none of your damn business but I am the perfect husband. A wonderful lover. Romantic.

I suppose you gave her beautiful gifts and flowers.

I always bought her the most beautiful card in the store.
A card? Whoopee!
It's the thought that counts.

Megan hurries into the office. Sally's nieces are busy with coloring books in the back office. Otherwise, it seems very quiet.
"Did I have any calls?"
"Not one person. How was your date?"

"Don't ask. I hope we get better results from the personal ad. It comes out this week."

Chapter Twenty-Eight

The personal ad is live on-line. Men start answering.

Her first date is in a sports bar.

The TV is blaring with the *Bears* game. Megan approaches a young muscle man, who is drinking a beer at the bar. He is wearing a blue shirt.

"Are you Chuck? I'm supposed to be meeting a man in a blue shirt."

"The one and only. Hey, are you Megan? Cool baby. You rock."

"There must be some misunderstanding here. I thought you'd be older. I was expecting someone a little more mature."

"You like the *Bears*?"

"Yes, I like them."

"We are set. We'll go to the game on Sunday. You lucked out tonight, baby."

"I can't go on Sunday. I have to go to a concert."

"Who's comin' in?"

"It's *Bach*."

"I love *Bach Turner Overdrive*! He starts singing "Takin' Care of Business…"

The ghost of Julius and Danny are sitting at the other end of the bar. He calls after Megan as she leaves.

If you like him, you could adopt him, you know.

On to the next date.

Megan is having coffee with a widower from her ad at a *Barnes and Noble* café.

"Yes, it was sad. I loved my wife. 20 wonderful years. Until she died -

He is tearing up.

- Halloween night. We were so close. It is very hard to be alone."

"Halloween? Boy, that was just a couple of months ago."

"Well, I did say I was a recent widower."

"I'm just thinking back to when you answered my ad. I think it was four weeks ago."

"Like I said, it is tough to be alone."

The ghost of Julius and Danny are sitting at an adjacent table having coffee. Danny is reading *Variety*. Julius is leafing through a book called, *Journeys Out of the Body*.

His wife must be spinning in her grave that he is dating so soon.

Danny disagrees. *I've met his wife. She was glad to get rid of him.*

Chapter Twenty-Nine

Sally comes into Megan's office.

"There's a man outside who wants to see you. His name is Stan."

"Stan? Oh, Stan. OK."

She remembers the boring dinner she had with him. Another disaster.

Stan comes in.

"I wanted to tell you what a great time I had the other night."

"Yes. It was nice to meet you."

"I thought maybe we could go out on Friday night. Or Saturday or Sunday."

"Stan, I don't think this is a fit between us."

"I bought you dinner, you know. Look, I just don't go around buying dinners for people. It cost me forty bucks."

Megan reaches behind her for her purse. "Here. I'll give you a complete refund."

Stan hesitates, then takes the money and puts it in his pocket.

"I'll give you a call in a week. Maybe you'll change your mind.

"I won't. Don't call."

The ghost of Julius and Danny are standing in the office and have been listening to the conversation. He turns to Danny.

Where do these idiots come from?

On to the next. The prospective dates keep calling from the personal ad. Nobody interesting so far.

Megan is having dinner with a distinguished looking, older man at the

International Club, an elegant, private restaurant in the *Drake Hotel*. They are seated by a window overlooking the lights on Lake Shore Drive and the city.

"I know it must is painful for you, but this is our second date and I'd like you to tell me a little about your late wife".

"My late wife? My wife is very much alive."

"You're married? It took two dates to tell me?"

"Yes. But I have an arrangement with my wife."

"I'm not comfortable with that."

"Give it a chance. My wife is going to love you. She can't wait to meet you. We'll take you on beautiful trips around the world."

"Trips? You're going to take me on trips? I'm in the travel business."

Megan grabs her purse and stands up.

"If you want to impress me, you and your wife are going to have to buy me a Mercedes SL500."

And as she walks away -

"Yellow. With a black convertible top."

The ghost of Julius and Danny are having dinner nearby. As Megan exits, they give each other a high five!

At home, Megan is taking off her makeup. Alex stands in the doorway.

"Mom, I know it's lonely for you without Dad around."

'It is, Alex."

"I'm a little worried about some of the men you are seeing. Do you know anything about them?"

She ignores the question.

"I always met them in a public place. And I always drive my own car."

"Still, I want you to be very careful, Mom."

In the morning, Megan is having her morning coffee in the den. She has a pad and she is writing a letter to God. She prays out loud.

"All That Is, God. Whoever You are up there. If You are up there. I need a miracle.

Send me a man I can love. Let him love me.

God! Are You out there?

I need a miracle."

The ghost of Julius, in a brocade robe, walks in from the kitchen with his coffee. Danny follows on his heels.

Nobody believes in miracles anymore. That's a waste of time. There's not one damn person she's praying to who listens.

They listen. They listen. But you got to be reasonable.

Chapter Thirty

Megan is jogging along the lake with Arlene.

"So far, the personal ads are not working. Maybe Linda is right. There is no one out there."

"Why don't you come with me to some of the personal growth groups I attend? We both could meet someone there."

"I'll try anything."

"The ghost of Julius is jogging along behind them."

Why don't you try to grow up?

Later that day, Megan is listening to the voice mail messages at the answer number for her personal ad.

"You have three messages. To hear the first message, press one."

Megan presses one.

"Hello beautiful. This is Harry. I read your ad and I loved it. We are perfect together. I like everything you like. Can't wait to hear from you. My number is 555 228 4090."

Megan writes the number down with a smile. He sounds nice.

"You now have two messages. To hear your next message, press one."

Megan presses one.

"This is Harry. I left you a message earlier. I was surprised I had not heard from you. We are perfect for each other. Please give me a call at 555 228 4090."

"You have one message left. To hear your message, press one."

Megan presses one.

"This is Harry. Who the hell do you think you are? You think you are too good for me, right? Look, Miss Snob, I'll get you for this. Call me. You have the number. And do it now or I'll track you down."

Megan drops the phone on its base abruptly. She is horrified.

She gets up and locks all the doors and windows in the house.

The ghost of Julius is sitting on the couch reading his newspaper. He looks up at Megan over his glasses.

Are you done with this or do we have to wait for Jack the Ripper to answer your ad?

Chapter Thirty-One

Danny has been called in for a Committee meeting.

The same group *of* shadowy white figures is sitting around a table with a white tablecloth. Danny is sitting at the table in his battered, old hat. The Chairman addresses him.

We want to apologize, Danny. We made a mistake giving you Julius for your first case.

That's OK. It's good practice for me.

Julius won't grow and be happy if he remains earth bound. We're thinking of sending in a replacement. Someone more experienced.

No, please. Give me a chance. I want to do it.

OK, Danny. We'll give you a little more time. But not much longer.

Back in the kitchen, Alex is leaving for his classes.

"Are you going out again tonight, Mom?"

"No, I will be home. Why?"

"It's pretty weird to have your mother dating all the time."

"I'm taking a break right now."

"Good. I was hoping I wouldn't have to see any of those guys at breakfast."

The ghost of Julius has been listening to the conversation.

Breakfast? Over my dead body. They were all losers.

Danny walks into the kitchen.

Nobody is a loser. We are all just playing our parts. And every single scene is important to our movie. And to each other's movie. It's a jigsaw puzzle.

What nonsense .I thought I told you to scram, loser .How come they let you come back?

If I can't bring you in, they will send in a heavy hitter.

I have things to do here. I am not leaving.

Danny remembers wistfully.

I had less aggravation when I was booking comics into the Catskills.

Chapter Thirty-Two

In desperation, Megan has confided in Arlene.

"Julius is still here. I can't see him or hear him but his voice is always in my head. He follows me everywhere. I hope I am not going crazy."

Arlene has a suggestion.

"I know of a psychic who is supposed to be great. Several of my friends swear by him. I'll make an appointment and take you to see him. Will you go?"

"I probably have to. Sometimes, I think I am losing my mind."

She calls her sister June for advice.

"What do you think, June? It feels spooky. But I am already spooked. And he charges $100."

June laughs.

"That's pretty cheap if he can get that voice of Julius out of your head. You never see him or actually hear him? It's just mental, right?"

"Exactly, although lately I have been talking back at him out loud. It is such a crazy thing. And after all this time, I don't think I am imagining it. And he did give me that stock tip."

"I think he is definitely around, Megan. I have read about such things. Just do it."

A week later, Megan is sitting in a dark room across from the psychic. He is wearing a red turban. His eyes are closed.

"Give me a moment to connect."

"Oh, yes. My guides are showing me your

husband, Julius. You are attached by a silver cord. He is floating above you."

"He is not floating. He's at home. He's in the office. He follows me everywhere I go. And I hear his voice in my head all the time."

"We must tell him to go to *The Light*. There is love there for him there. He must let go of his earthly life. The silver cord must be cut."

"Look, I'm willing. I want him to leave. He won't go. How do we cut the cord?"

"I'm going higher. I am asking my angels now."

A long pause then his eyes pop open. "This is more difficult that I thought. They are telling me you both are holding on to the cord. You are as responsible as he is. We need several sessions to work on this."

Arlene is waiting for Megan outside the office in her car. They drive off.

"So did he tell you when you were going to meet someone?"

"We never got to that. I just paid $100.00 for him to tell me Julius was still around. Like I didn't already know."

"That's all he said?"

"He said something about having to cut a silver cord."

The ghost of Julius is sitting in the back of the car. Danny is with him.

That guy in the turban is a nut. Don't give him any more money.

Danny adds his opinion.

He's right. Even without your awareness, both of you are holding on to each other.

That's bull. We love each other.

I am growing.I have things to make up to her. I've been too hard on her.
It's too late for this time, Julius. Maybe you can do it in another lifetime. Not now.

Chapter Thirty-Three

There is a big sign outside a large room in a hotel.

"FREE INTRODUCTION TO WHOLE LIVING FORUM HERE."

Megan and Arlene walk in and take seats. There are over a hundred people in the audience. The Workshop Presenter is at the podium. He is dressed in blue jeans and a sweatshirt.

"Do you think this will help us find a good man?"

"You never know. I see lots of men here. Shush. It's starting."

"Welcome everyone. Are you ready for a new life?"

The crowd is quiet.

"OK. I'm going to ask you again. Are you ready to change your life? Let's hear it loud and clear!"

The crowd shouts, "Yesss!"

"Here is some shocking news for you. Listen carefully. NOTHING that has happened in your life up until now matters. NOTHING! You've been HIDING behind old, destructive stories. EVERY ONE OF YOU IS SIMPLY SURVIVING rather than BEING ALIVE. Are you ready to start LIVING?"

The crowd shouts, "Yessss!"

Megan and Arlene are leaving after the presentation.

"So what do you think, Megan?

"I don't know. I think it's a little over the top for me."

The ghost of Julius is following them out of the room.

Did you see that, Danny? More money going out to snake oil salesmen. All this self-improvement junk and nobody improves.

Chapter Thirty-Four

As Megan is walking into the office, the whole staff is standing around Sally's desk. She is on the telephone.

"Yes, I want him paged. It is urgent. Mr. Edward O'Malley. He is at the Mexicana boarding gate to Ixtapa."

Catherine is scared.

"I thought it was the right city."

Sally is very annoyed.

"He is going to the *Ixtapan Spa* outside of Mexico City. You wrote him a ticket to *Ixtapa*, a city on the ocean 600 miles away."

Linda tries to console Catherine.

"Everybody makes mistakes. But this is a very big one."

Harriet adds her wisdom.

"This is just what Shelley told me. This is why he said people were booking on the Internet. Shelley says –"

Catherine sits down and covers her eyes.

"I want you to know that my intentions were of the very finest."

Sally is still on the phone. She chides Catherine.

"*The Ixtapan Spa* is on the top of a mountain. Where did you think they would put an airport? Hello. Hello. Have you found him?"

"They found him."

Catherine looks up, relieved.

"Actually, I was wondering where they would put an airport."

Sally has Mr. O'Malley on the phone.

"Oh, Mr. O'Malley. There has been a tiny

change to your flight arrangements. We have found a more direct way to get to the spa. Go to the ticket agent and pick up a new ticket to Mexico City. We'll have a limo waiting to take you to the spa when you arrive."

(Pause)

"Yes, this is a much faster way. Oh, you are entirely welcome. Have a wonderful time now."

Megan sits down in relief.

"Wow! That was a squeaker! Good work, Sally."

Catherine is now crying loudly.

"This has been such a terrible day."

"It's OK, Catherine It's been solved. I am just glad they found him."

"It's not only this. Blackie is being operated on for cancer. I took him in this morning."

Chapter Thirty-Five

Danny is following the ghost of Julius down Michigan Avenue. They stop to look at the window display at *Tiffany*.

What are we doing here?

I've decided cards are not enough. I'm going to buy something special for Megan.

You can't make things up to her. You're dead.

They enter the store. The ghost of Julius approaches a salesman.

I'd like to see something in diamond earrings.

The salesman does not look up.

Excuse me. Did you hear what I said? I want to see some diamond earrings.

The salesman walks away. The ghost of Julius looks at Danny. He realizes the salesman can't hear him.

Let's go, Julius . You've got to give up. This life is over.

Chapter Thirty-Six

A police car, a paddy wagon and an ambulance, all with lights flashing, are in front of Annie's building. One of the policemen is Eric. He and another policeman are taking Nick, who is handcuffed and struggling, out of the building and pushing him into the paddy wagon.

"Get in there, you pervert. You can't keep beating women up. You've got an arrest warrant out on you for the last one."

Linda speeds up in her car. Two paramedics are carrying Annie out on a stretcher. They open the back door of the ambulance. Linda runs over to her. Eric follows.

"I think she's okay except for one arm, but we're taking her to the hospital to make sure. Are you the one who called us?"

"Yes. She called me at home. She was hysterical and said she was hurt. What happened?"

"This guy has a record of assault a mile long. He won't be bothering her or anybody else for a long time. You can bet on that."

Linda takes Annie's hand. She is lying on the stretcher and crying softly.

"I'm going with you. You're going to be okay, Annie. I'll be right here. I'm with you."

She climbs into the back of the ambulance with Annie. It leaves with the siren blaring.

In the morning, the women are standing around Linda as she tells them what happened.

They are all shaken by the news.

"She was lucky. It could have been a lot worse. Her arm may be broken. They were doing an X- Ray. After that black eye, I was afraid of something like this."

Catherine is teary.

"So many bad things are happening. Blackie with cancer. And now Annie. What can we do for her?"

Megan is resolute.

"We'll support her. The whole team. You were so good to her, Linda."

Linda shrugs off the compliment.

"Women have to help each other. We're all we've got. I'm moving her in with me for a while. Then, when she is better, she can go back to her apartment. I'll have the whole place cleaned up. He will not be there ever again."

And they do. Everyone has a day to bring Annie dinner and keep her company. She is feeling much better. The break was not severe so she is in a soft cast and comes back to work in a few weeks. She can talk on the telephone and hunt and peck on her computer with her right hand.

But the troubles continue.

Catherine is walking into the office carrying a large box. Megan is standing by Sally's desk in the front of the office.

"What's in the box, Catherine?"

"Blackie."

Linda looks up from her computer.

"You brought a cat to work?"

"He is too sick to stay home alone. He'll be no trouble. He just lies there."

And then, tearfully -

"Is it okay, Megan?"

Megan hesitates, glances in the box and turns away looking pained. She answers,

"It's okay, Catherine. Blackie is welcome."

Chapter Thirty-Seven

Arlene has taken Megan to a large *A Course in Miracles* workshop. The Facilitator is reading from the text of the course.

"If we really understand this passage, it could change our lives."

(Reverent pause)

Nothing outside yourself can save you. Nothing outside yourself can bring you peace.

Megan and Arlene are talking about it during the coffee break.

"I love this, Arlene. It really speaks to me."

"Me too. I am so glad you like it. We'll start attending regularly."

George is a Robert Redford look-alike. He is walking out of the crowd toward Megan. She sees "lights" all around him.

"Well, hello there. I saw you come in. My name is George."

Megan is flustered.

"I'm Megan. And, oh, this is my friend, Arlene."

George nods at Arlene and then turns his full attention back to Megan. His smile is dazzling.

"I heard you mention you were going to attend the follow up groups."

"Yes, I'd like to. Are you?"

"Definitely."

There are many group members at the next study group of *A Course in Miracles*. The meeting has ended, but some are still sitting at a round table having cake and coffee.

Arlene is talking.

"I think it's hard to meet people who are compatible. I've been divorced for three years."

George agrees.

"I'm not ready. I've been divorced only six months. I'm on a year sabbatical from teaching and I want to write – and have some fun."

Another woman adds, "I believe in fate. When you are supposed to meet – the right person arrives."

A young man says, "I agree. I met my girlfriend in a grocery store. We had the exact same items in our carts. I took that as a sign."

Megan laughs "That is a sign for sure. Suppose you meet someone and you see lights all around him?"

Another woman answers. "I would think that was a sign."

George adds to the conversation.

"I know what I'm looking for. I don't want any more mistakes."

Megan is curious. "What are you looking for?"

George looks directly at Megan with a little smile as he answers.

"Someone not too young. Pretty. Smart. Independent. A little crazy but basically a down-to-earth woman who can cook."

The ghost of Julius arrives in time to hear the end of the conversation.

Don't expect much cooking from Megan, unless you want to count Chinese take-out left overs in the microwave.

The group is leaving. Everyone is hugging

good-bye.

"See you all next week. It was great."

George and Megan are the last ones to leave. He gives Megan a long hug.

"We ought to get together for dinner sometime."

Megan, not able to hide her excitement, answers almost too quickly.

"I would love that."

They stand there an extra moment, just smiling at each other. There is clearly electricity in the air.

Chapter Thirty- Eight

Four men are wiping the Lincoln down after it has been washed. The ghost of Julius is walking around the car, inspecting the job. He points, with his cigar, to a spot that needs attention.

One of the men stops, looks up at the sky, shrugs – and then goes over and rubs the spot with his cloth.

Megan is on her cell phone talking to her sister, June.

"My car is almost ready so I'll call you later. But June, this is the man I have been waiting for. This is the ONE, June."

She turns to the men as she gets in the car, leaving a nice tip.

"Thanks, guys."

The ghost of Julius is sitting with Danny in the back seat as she drives off. He flips his cigar ash out the window. Danny is fanning himself.

Keep that window open. Don't you know second hand smoke can kill you? I told them I wanted a non smoker."

The ghost of Julius opens *The Wall Street Journal* and looks up over his half-glasses at Megan who is driving.

If THIS is the man you've been waiting for, we are in big trouble.

Chapter Thirty-Nine

George and Megan are having dinner and drinking Chianti in a local Italian restaurant with checkered red tablecloths.

"I'm glad you could make it at the last minute. I hate eating alone."

"I'm pretty spontaneous."

"I like that."

"George, you said you have studied the Course for years."

"Yes, it has really helped me over some rough spots. The divorce. And I have a little problem with depression. It comes and goes."

"I can't believe how honest you are."

"It's funny. As soon as I met you, I knew I could tell you anything."

Megan goes through the week in a happy glow.

Saturday morning, her doorbell is ringing at her house.

It is George.

"Is Alex home? I was in the neighborhood and I thought it would be nice to meet him and talk about philosophy."

"He sure is. Come on in."

George and Alex are in the den reading together and talking intently.

George has left. Megan is cooking. Alex comes in to the kitchen.

"He's a nice guy, Mom. Did you know that George has a *Doctorate* in philosophy?"

"Yes, I did. You like him?"

"He's cool. Really smart. He can come over whenever he wants." Megan smiles.

Chapter Forty

Megan and George are riding in George's convertible. The top is down. It is a beautiful, sunny day.

"I think my brother divorced his wife because she refused to serve rutabagas with turkey."

Megan throws her head back and laughs.

"I ALWAYS serve rutabagas with turkey."

"How did I know that about you?"

The ghost of Julius and Danny are riding in the back seat.

I don't know who writes this guy's material, but it stinks. I wish they'd put the top up. That wind is murdering my sinuses.

And another date.

Megan and George are viewing *SUE*, the dinosaur at the Field Museum. George is imitating the skeleton's stance. Megan snaps his picture. They both crack up laughing. The ghost of Julius and Danny are watching.

She hasn't laughed like that with me for a long time.

What do you think happened?

I don't know. I got too serious about life.

The relationship happily continues.

It is another breezy summer day. George and Megan are running along the lake path at Oak Street beach. They are back dropped by the panorama of the skyline of Chicago.

"I'll race you to the beach."

"I'll give you a head start. Go."

He quickly catches up with her. Then they stumble and laughing, roll over together on the beach by the water. He holds her, looking at her intently.

"Are we in a scene from *"From Here to Eternity?"*

"There are no waves."

"We don't need waves."

George kisses her. Then, pulls back and sits up.

"God, I wish I was in love with you."

"Maybe you are."

For a long moment, George holds her.

The ghost of Julius and Danny walk up to the couple on the beach and look down on them. Julius is annoyed at the scene.

Please.

The budding romance continues.

It is a balmy evening. George and Megan are strolling along *The Magnificent Mile* on Michigan Avenue. They are holding hands. They stop to admire a red dress in the *Neiman Marcus* window.

"That dress is you."

"It's beautiful. I bet it's expensive."

"Come on. I am going to buy you that dress."

"Are you kidding me?"

"No. Come on. It's got your name on it."

The ghost of Julius and Danny are not far behind the couple.

Make sure you get her the shoes that go

with it, cheapskate!

Chapter Forty-One

The women are arriving into the lunchroom. They sit down and start unwrapping the deli sandwiches.

Harriet feels sad.

"How terrible about Blackie dying. Catherine is devastated. I wonder when she'll come back to work."

Linda is not so sympathetic.

"It's only a cat, for God's sakes. And it was 18 years old."

Annie is sitting with a sling on her arm.

"You just don't get it. Blackie was her family. She's all alone in her house now."

Linda considers this and looks thoughtful.

"It's pretty sad when you can't even count on a male cat."

Megan arrives in the room. She seems to be very distracted lately. She sits down and opens her sandwich.

Linda asks her a business question.

"Megan, what have you heard about the new *Princess* ship? Megan? Are you listening?"

Megan suddenly comes back to earth.

"Oh, I hear it's beautiful."

Sally wisely comments.

"Leave her alone. She's in love."

Annie is wistful.

"I was like that. I just hope she doesn't get hurt."

Linda adds –
"She probably will."

The women go back to their desks. Megan and Annie are about to leave when Eric arrives in his uniform, hat in hand.

"I just wanted to check in on you, Annie. How are you feeling?"

"I'm better, Eric. That is so nice of you. I appreciate all your help."

"Let me know if you need anything, OK?"

Eric waves and leaves the office.

Megan approves. "Now, there's a good guy."

"There were a lot of good things about Nick, too."

"Everyone has good in them. But when there's more bad than good, we have to move on."

Chapter Forty-Two

George and Megan on sitting on a couch in front of a fireplace in the *Ritz Carlton* lounge. George has his arm around her. She is wearing the red dress he bought her. A piano is playing softly nearby.

"That was a wonderful dinner. Thank you, George."

"God! You look beautiful in the firelight."

"It's my new dress."

George shakes his head.

"No, it's you. You have the most intense eyes. Sometimes I feel like you can see into my soul."

Megan teases him. "I can. So, be careful."

"I know you would never hurt me. That is so important to me."

The ghost of Julius is stoking the fire in his white dinner jacket. Danny is with him. He turns to Megan.

You're not buying this crap, are you? Somebody give me a break here.

George continues. "I have a little surprise for you. I hope you will like it."

"What is it?"

George reaches into his pocket and pulls out a key. "I booked us a suite here."

Megan and George leave quickly.

The ghost of Julius and Danny sit down on the couch.

Well, have you had enough?

How could she do this to me, Danny? I

never thought she'd cheat on me.

    She's not cheating. You're dead. Remember? If you really love her, why would you want her to be alone?

    Danny's cell phone is ringing.

    I know. I know. Don't be so impatient. I think he's coming around.

    I wish you would stop talking to those people on the phone and just talk to me.

    The Higher Ups are in on this now. They said to tell you it's time for you to come home.

    I don't have a home anymore. I'm miserable.

    You would be happy on the other side.

    I wouldn't have Megan.

    You don't have Megan now.

    Then, more kindly - *You will be with her again. Someday.*

    Are you sure about that?

    I hope so. The Committee will decide.

Chapter Forty-Three

George and Megan enter the suite. There is a luxurious living room with the view at night of Lake Michigan out the window. Megan is walking around, visibly nervous with the thrill of it.

George takes her hand, leading her.
In the bedroom of the suite, George removes the red dress and places it on a chair.
He is a tender but strong lover. Megan never remembers sex as powerful as this. The couple is lying in bed. They don't seem to be able to get enough of each other.
After more sex, George is stroking her hair.
"I love you, George."
"I love you, Megan. You are so important to me. You're like my family. Like the sister I never had."
Megan sits straight up in bed with a surprised look.
"SISTER?"
"Did you say sister?"

Chapter Forty-Four

Megan is on the Stairmaster. The ghost is standing in front of her, wagging his cigar at her. Danny is with him.

That guy is taking you for a ride. I don't want him to hurt you.

Megan decides to communicate with her deceased husband, directly, for the first time.

"You are trying to sabotage me."

Look, I want you to be happy. I'm even willing to look out for someone for you.

"I have someone."

He's wrong. He's using you.

"I love him, Julius."

He doesn't love you.

"Go away. Let me be happy."

The ghost of Julius and Danny are walking away.

You got to stop interfering.

That bum is going to break her heart. You talk to her. Do something.

She has to find her own way. We all do.

A few evenings later, the doorbell is ringing. Megan answers the door in her bathrobe. George is standing in the pouring rain. It is 10 PM.

"I hope I didn't wake you."

"No, not at all. I was just watching the news. Come in. You're all wet."

"I feel very depressed tonight."

They sit down on the couch. Megan puts her arms around him.

"I don't know how I made it without you."

"You don't have to make it without me."

"Look, would it be okay if I stayed here tonight on the couch?"

"Sure. I'll get you some pillows and a blanket. We'll talk in the morning."

Later that night, Megan is in bed. There is a tapping on her door. It is George. He is holding his pillow.

"I've got a bad case of the jitters. Can I just lie down next to you?"

"Come on. Get into bed."

She pulls back the covers. He gets into bed with her.

"You always make me feel so safe."

George puts his arms around her and falls asleep immediately. Megan is wide awake, listening to the rain.

The ghost of Julius and Danny are standing in the hall outside the bedroom. Julius is upset.

That guy is sleeping in my bed!

The next morning, Megan and George are having breakfast. Alex was gone for an early class when they woke up.

"George, you seem to be going through a bad time right now. Why don't you stay with us for a while?"

"What would Alex think? Although, I could sleep on the couch in the den."

"He would think it was fine. He likes you".

George answers eagerly. "I'll go pick up my computer and some of my things. I always feel so much better when I'm with you."

Chapter Forty-Five

George is sitting at the desk in Megan's home office. His computer is open in front of him. He calls Megan at the office.

"I'm not coming to the meeting tonight. I'm going to a movie."

"Okay."

"Look, Megan, don't mention that I've been depressed and staying with you. I don't want the group to feel sorry for me."

"I won't. I'll see you later then."

A while later, Alex walks in the front door with his books. He drops his backpack on the floor and throws his coat on the banister.

In the kitchen, Alex opens the refrigerator and takes things out for a sandwich. Then, he remembers he has to call a friend and picks up the kitchen phone. As he is about to dial, he hears George's voice on the extension in the upstairs office.

The lights are dim. George is speaking on the telephone in hushed tones.

"I've been in London for two weeks doing some research. I miss you too. I'll be home by this weekend. Look, I have to hang up. Bye, darling."

He hangs up the phone and calls downstairs. "Is that you, Alex? Aren't you home early?"

"Yeah. A lab got canceled. But I'm leaving again. You can go back to your call from

London."

George looks scared. He's been caught.

Alex gets his bike and goes to his mother's office.

"How long is George going to stay with us?"

"I don't know exactly. Why?"

"He ties up the phone line. He needs his own computer connection."

"I thought you liked George."

"He's okay, but I am starting to develop my own philosophy. People are not always what they seem to be."

Megan is arriving home after work. She pulls her car in the driveway, next to George's car. George is loading his computer and some suitcases into his car. It is raining again.

Megan jumps out of her car.

"Where are you going?"

"It is time for me to get back to my own place, Megan. I need to be quiet and do some writing. By the way, last night I couldn't sleep so I went into the garage and fixed your car. It won't stall anymore."

"That was nice. But then, you are just leaving without talking to me?"

"Of course not. I wrote you a note. I'll call you or call me."

George is pulling out of the driveway. Megan shouts after him.

"Your phone is always on voice mail."

He doesn't hear her. He is gone.

The ghosts of Julius and Danny have been standing in the rain in the driveway. He turns to Danny.

Good riddance! I hope this one is over.

That evening, A *Course in Miracles* study group is arriving. Arlene is in the meeting room kitchen with Megan, setting up the coffee.

"Is George coming tonight?"

"I don't know. I hope so."

One of the women from the group is talking to another in the hall as they arrive.

"George won't be here tonight again. He called me from London. He's been there for two weeks, doing research."

Megan and Arlene look at each other.

"George told her he was in London?"

Chapter Forty-Six

The door is closed to Megan's office. She is talking to her sister, June, on the telephone.

"I haven't heard from him and his phone is on voicemail as usual."

"I've decided to write him a letter. I want a commitment from him. But, June, suppose he turns me down? I'll die."

"At least then I will know. But I don't think he will. This man is in love with me."

Megan sits at her desk and writes a long letter, seals it and walks out.

Sally puts her call on hold.

"Where are you going in such a hurry?"

Megan is beaming.

"I'm going to mail a letter and then I am going shopping."

First stop is at *Victoria's Secret.*

Megan is looking at a diaphanous white robe – then a black nightgown. Then some black underwear. She is checking out with the cashier.

Next stop is *Bloomingdales.*

She is holding up red satin sheets. She rubs her face in the pillowcase dreamily. The ghost of Julius is watching her.

Megan is paying for the red satin sheets.

Are you kidding me? With the way you keep house? Who's going to iron satin sheets?

After her shopping spree, she stops home, and then decides to visit Arlene.

Alex is studying in the den.

"I'm going over to Arlene's house. I'll be back about four o'clock."

"Okay."

"Do you have her telephone number?"

"Somewhere."

"I am writing her number down and leaving it right by the phone."

"Okay."

"In case of an emergency."

"You mean in case George calls. You know, I think he's a player, Mom."

"Don't be ridiculous. Let me know if he calls right away."

The next day, she is back at work.

At lunch the girls are talking.

"Isn't Megan having lunch?"

Annie answers "She says she isn't hungry."

Harriet, as usual, has the answer. "Maybe she's coming down with something. Shelley says everyone in his office is sick with something."

Catherine disagrees.

"She's grieving. I know what that's like. Has she heard from George?"

Sally says, "Take a look at her face. Can't you tell he hasn't called her?"

Linda adds, "That bastard. They're all bastards."

Megan has come home from the office She is still wearing her coat as she picks up the mail from the floor at the front door. She opens a letter and reads it.

"Damn! I don't believe this."

Alex is coming down the stairs.

"Believe what?"

"Sidney sent me a letter of apology he got from the Veteran's Administration in Washington and a $400 invoice for legal services."

"You know, Mom, Mrs. Maroni, next door, told me there was a man who was asking questions about you. Maybe it was the VA."

"I don't know. Whatever they found out they turned me down for benefits anyway."

Megan is on watch to hear from George but no calls, no answer to her calls, or her letter. She is trying to keep things normal.

Megan is leaving the office. She talks to Sally from the front door.

"I'm running over to American Visa Service. I should be back in an hour."

"Okay."

"You have their number over there?"

"Yes, we have the number."

"Call me if I have any messages, OK?"

"We'll call you right away."

At the end of the day, Megan and Arlene are jogging along the lake. It is a cold and gray.

"You just can't wait by phones night and day. He's a smart man. If he wants to see you, he'll find you."

" It feels good to get out in the air. I'm glad you pushed me."

Chapter Forty-Seven

Arlene is right. The next day, George walks into Megan's office. She is on the phone with a client.

She ends the call quickly.

"Hello, George."

George closes the door and sits down.

"That was a beautiful letter."

"Thank you."

"You know I wouldn't hurt you."

"I hope not."

"I thought I had made it perfectly clear to you that I was not ready for a relationship."

"We already have a relationship."

George gets up and walks over to Megan.

"I just want to be friends, Megan. I can't handle the responsibility of a commitment."

"I can't just be your friend."

"I was thinking we should plan a workshop on a ship. *A Spiritual Seminar at Sea.* Wouldn't that be fun?"

Megan stands to face him.

"I don't want to be your travel agent. I wanted to have a life with you."

"Let's pretend you never wrote the letter. I want you back the way you were before."

George pulls her to him and holds her. She is crying now.

"Please don't cry, Megan. I love you. But like family."

Megan pulls away and pushes him.

"I am not your family. Leave now. Just go."

The ghost of Julius and Danny are standing in the corner of the room. He turns to

Danny.
> Very touching. What a complete jerk.
> Danny shakes his head.
> For once, I agree with you.

Chapter Forty-Eight

Megan has been on the telephone with her sister, June. She has been crying.

The ghost of Julius is sitting on the couch carefully lighting his cigar.

"Well, at least I know. I feel like someone died. And that someone is me."

After a pause -

"No. I can't just be his friend. I can't go back to the way things were."

The ghost of Julius gets up to turn on the TV evening news. He turns to Megan.

Did I or did I not tell you this guy was a bum?

Megan starts crying again.

"Go away. Just leave me alone."

After a restless night, Megan calls the office to tell them she will not be in today. She has a lot of errands.

Megan is returning the gown and the other lingerie at the cashier's counter at *Victoria's Secret.*

Megan is returning the sheets to a salesperson at *Bloomingdales.* The ghost of Julius and Danny are with her.

"Do you have a receipt?"

"I can't find it. Can't I get a refund without it?"

"I can give you a refund, but the sheets are on sale now. With no receipt, I can only refund you at the sale price."

"OK. I still want to return them."

The ghost turns to Danny. *This is a perfect example of why I never had money.*

Next stop is the *Salvation Army.*

Megan gets out of her car and walks into the store carrying the red dress in a plastic garment bag.

Megan comes out without the dress, gets into the car and drives off. The ghost is in the back seat.

You gave a perfectly good dress away? It had a lot of wear left in it.

That evening, Megan is preparing dinner. Alex is sitting on a stool in the kitchen with her.

"You mean George won't be coming over anymore?"

"No. I broke things off with him."

"How can you just give up a friend?"

"It's heartbreaking, Alex. Maybe when you get older you'll understand."

(She is crying now)

Alex comes over to her and hugs her.

"Please don't cry, Mom. I'm still here."

Megan goes back to stirring a pot on the stove. Sniffling.

Mom?

What?

"You're not going to start talking about us moving again, are you?"

"No, Alex. Maybe someday. But for now, we're staying right here. This is our home."

Chapter Forty-Nine

Megan is back at her desk which is piled up with papers in stacks. She is preparing her records for her accountant who will be in this week.

Sally knocks on the door.

"There is a woman who wants to talk to you outside here."

"Can't anyone else take care of her? I'm trying to get all these records in order. Who is she?"

"Her name is Helen. I've never seen her before. She says it is personal."

"Personal? I can't imagine. Well, send her in."

Helen is a pleasant looking, middle aged woman, with gray hair and very bright, blue eyes. She is dressed nicely in a tailored, black pantsuit. She comes in, closes the door, and sits down.

She starts the conversation immediately.

"I have come to see you after hearing that you are a lovely woman with a teen age son and a recent widow. Otherwise, I would not bother contacting you."

Yes?

"I have also heard that you have been dating my husband, George."

Megan cannot conceal her shock.

'Your husband? He told me he was divorced."

"He is not. We have been married for over 20 years, despite some serious mental issues.

But there is more to the story.

We live in Seattle and have three children.

Last year, I inherited a sizable amount of money from my deceased father. George forged my name on documents and disappeared with many thousands of dollars of my money. There is a warrant for his arrest for Grand Larceny.

After becoming impatient with the police, I hired a private investigator. They found him here. He has been arrested, is presently in your Cook County Jail and is waiting for extradition back to Seattle. The investigator also turned up the information that he has been seeing you, even living at your home."

Megan feels like she is going to pass out.

"What about the things he said about being a professor of Philosophy with a Ph.D? He told me he was on a sabbatical leave."

"He has a brilliant mind and is very well self-educated in that area but he dropped out of college. Also, because of mental illness. He has been working as the chief mechanic for a large car agency in Seattle for years."

The disbelief Megan is feeling is overwhelming. She cannot speak.

Helen goes on.

"I am very sorry to give you this terrible news. But when the investigator talked to some of your neighbors and they said what a wonderful woman you are and how you cared for your very ill husband, so tenderly, I was sure that he deceived you. He is charming and a talented pathological liar."

Helen stands but does not offer her hand.

"I felt that as a woman who also been very hurt by him, I owed it to you. I'm leaving for the airport now. This has been hard for me to do. I wish you luck and that you find a good person who deserves you."

All Megan can say is "Thank you, Helen."

The ghost of Julius and Danny have been listening in the corner of the office. Even Julius has nothing to say.

Chapter Fifty

A few hours later, Megan was on the telephone with her sister, June.

She, of course, was as shocked. She couldn't believe it. And she had some questions Megan had not thought about.

"You are on the computer all the time. Did you ever Google him?"

Mega had to search her memory.

"I think I did the first time I met him but nothing came up. I think I assumed I had misspelled his name. After that, I was so besotted with him, I never thought about it."

"I wonder how they found him. Even the cleverest criminals slip up. Were there any clues at all, now that you think back?"

"I probably will never know. A couple of things that I did not pay much attention. He paid cash for everything. And his cell number changed several times. Maybe prepaid phones."

"Anyway, when I finally calm down and process this, it will be easier to just forget about him. That woman really did me a big favor. It's going to take me some time. But you know, I was only with him about four months."

"She certainly was kind to contact you. And brave. Few people would do that."

Megan arrived late the next day. She was not finished with the records for the accountant. It was a good distraction.

The women were having Chinese food today. They are putting out paper plates.

There was a big elephant in the room.

They had heard about the mystery woman and noticed that Megan's face was white as a sheet when she left to go home.

Catherine starts the conversation.
"I know how you feel, Megan. I don't know how long it's going to take me to get over Blackie's death."

"Death is different. When someone dies, the hope is gone."
Sally asks, "And if the person is still here?"
"There is always that secret foolish thought that someday – someday – he'll wake up and say, "What? – Was I crazy? I love her."

Megan continues –
"But that is not going to happen to me. I am going to tell you about that woman who visited yesterday with the understanding that it is strictly confidential. We are a team here. I trust every one of you."
They are passing around the cartons of food.

That statement just hangs in the air.

Megan finally speaks. Her voice is shaky and she is trying not to cry.
"I am still very raw but here are the bare bones of what she told me. I can't say much more because I am still in shock."
"She is George's wife. He is not divorced. They live in Seattle. He stole a great deal of money from her and disappeared. He is in jail

now. Every single thing he told me about himself was a lie. He is being extradited back for trial"

No one can speak.

Then, in unison, they get up and together, surround Megan in their arms.

The phones are ringing in the outer office. No one answers.

Chapter Fifty-One

The next morning, Megan is meeting with her accountant.

"You have to make a difficult decision here."

"I know, Jeffrey. I'm thinking about selling the agency."

"Selling? That's not what I had in mind, Megan. I'm sorry to tell you the agency is not worth anything."

"No one buys a small company that has been in the red for three years. You've been carrying it with your own money."

"You're not suggesting I close the agency, are you?"

Jeffrey stands to make his point.

"Yes, I am afraid I am. The day of the small, neighborhood travel agency is over. Your lease is up in two months. Don't renew it."

"What would I do with myself? What about my staff?"

Jeffrey answers kindly.

"Save yourself, Megan. Your staff will make their own way."

"I have to think about this."

"Your lease is up. Think fast".

Jeffrey gets up and leaves with his papers.

The ghost of Julius has been standing in his white dinner jacket with his cigar in his teeth. He walks forward and wags his cigar at Megan, scattering ashes all over her desk.

There is nothing to think about. You heard what he said. Just get out! It is time for you to grow up!

She stands up behind her desk and faces the ghost of Julius.

"I am grown up. And it is time for you to listen to your own advice. It's time for you to get out."

The ghost of Julius is looking with surprise at a coiled silver cord in his hand. Megan takes a scissors out of her desk and cuts the cord between them. Then he looks back at Megan.

What's this?

"I've cut the cord. Good-bye, Julius."

Danny struggles into the room carrying two bulging suitcases.

We're done here, Julius. Let's go. And stay right behind me this time.

Megan is sitting quietly at her desk now. She looks exhausted but peaceful.

Not so fast, buddy. I have something to say to this lady before we go. He swallows hard.

Megan, I know I have been a burden in your life and even in this half-life I've been in, but I want you to know I love you and I'm sorry. Danny says we may be together again someday. I'm going to make it up to you. I promise.

She can't hear you anymore, Julius.

She can't?

No. But love is always heard by the heart.
So, she knows.
I'm going to find a way to get back here.
You'll see.

The white boardroom in the sky comes into view.

Danny is sitting at the table. The Committee is clapping.

The Chairman speaks.

Good work, Danny. We have a new booking for you. But I'm warning you. This is tough one.

You don't let a person sit down for a minute in this place.

Chapter Fifty-Two

Megan has called her staff together for a meeting.

"So, I have no choice. We close in two months. Please complete the trips you have immediately. Don't accept any more bookings unless they are immediate. If you need time off, to interview for other jobs, take it. We'll cover for each other."

She pauses. Megan's voice catches "Like we've always done."

There is silence.

Chapter Fifty-Three

Megan had to agree with Jeffrey. It was a shocking revelation but the only practical solution. The day of the neighborhood agency was over.

Many had already closed because of disruption around the world. And as the Internet came roaring in, people found it easy to book and compare prices on domestic travel on their own.

She was not prepared for the physical work involved in closing or the emotional impact it would have on her.

After she notified her landlord, the dismantling was staggering.

Jeffrey came over to advise what documents she had to keep and suggested she keep her corporation active. Commissions from overseas could take months to arrive. He changed her address to her home and also with her bank.

The agency had many thousands of files and brochures. She called a junk mover to dispose of all of it.

Three huge men with a large truck emptied the office in a day. They delivered her safe and some filing cabinets to her basement at home.

Good Will was glad to accept and pick up all the furniture and computers.

Much more to do with her airline agreements and to return all unused ticket stock and printers. Her airline software contract had to be canceled.

More things to do kept popping up. A change of address for the postoffice. She had to resign from many travel agency organizations who all charged yearly dues.

Finally it was done. The office was empty and cleaned.

It felt like a funeral. Megan and her staff were all crying. They had been a big help in the transition. They hugged each other. It was the end of a long relationship.

Chapter Fifty-Four

It wasn't until she locked the door and delivered the keys to the landlord, that the emotional impact hit her.

A year ago, she had many roles. Wife, caretaker, mother, lover and business owner.

The only role left was mother. Alex was so involved in college, activities and friends, he no longer needed much mothering.

She had no place to go but home.

Nothing left to do.

She poured herself a glass of wine and sat in her big chair in the den.

"Who is Megan now? What did she want?" Nothing came to mind.

After the disastrous relationship with George, she was not interested in a romantic partner.

She and Julius had traveled the world. There was no place she wanted to see and no one she wanted to travel with.

She was financially secure. With all his complaining, Julius had seen to that. No money worries.

As usual, in any crisis, she called her sister. June lived 1000 miles away in rural upstate New York.

Should she move there? June was busy with her husband and children and there was little to do there.

And Alex was firmly entrenched in Chicago. She had promised they would not move.

June was up to date with all the details of closing the agency. She was not surprised at the call.

She listened for a long time. She was very involved with all the losses Megan had endured in the past year.

Her final words to Megan were a quote from their mother.

"She used to tell us, when you don't know what to do, do nothing. Let time pass."

Megan realized she was trying to fill in all the spaces and it was too soon.

She finished her wine and walked into the kitchen.

Alex would be home for dinner soon.

THREE MONTHS LATER –

The office staff is together for a farewell lunch. It is an unseasonably warm, sunny day. The women are seated at a sidewalk, upscale restaurant in downtown Chicago. There is a round table under a festive umbrella. The waiter is passing out menus.

The office is officially closed. Sally took her nieces to Walt Disney World and is starting a new job in a large commercial agency next week.

They are reminiscing about their years together.

Sally says,

"My favorite story is the woman who insisted that I book her on a driving vacation from one Hawaiian Island to another. She hung up on me when I told her there was no road."

Harriet and Shelley are still discussing what she should do next.

Harriet adds

"What about the group that canceled because I never told them a cruise was on a ship? Shelley couldn't believe it."

Linda finally got her big divorce settlement and is taking a World Cruise on the Queen Mary II.

Linda looks up from the menu she is studying.

"Don't forget the parrot that shrieked obscenities on Delta all the way to Florida."

Annie is going back to teaching kindergarten. She is dating Eric, the policeman, now. After all the accidents he has covered on his job, he hates motorcycles.

"I'll never forget how good all of you were to me."

"Everyone helped each other. There was so much love in the office."

She takes out a handkerchief and wipes tears from her eyes.

"We even loved the customers."

Catherine has applied to the Peace Corps. She is interviewing today.

Suddenly, the waiter comes to the table with a bottle of wine for Megan.

The gentleman at the next table has sent it with his compliments and his card.

The man smiles and raises his glass to Megan. She smiles back. The women look at him and then back at her with approving glances.

Lunch is over. The waiter is bringing the bill to the table.

A few months ago I would have jumped at the chance to meet a guy like that. But not now. Maybe much later.

Megan is signing the check and the women are gathering their things to leave.

I replaced the roof. I sold my old Lincoln and Julius' sports car. The power always scared me. I'm looking for a small, reliable car. - and this year I will decide what flowers I want in my garden – and about everything else.

Megan stops on the way out to say thanks to the attractive man.

"What a nice thing to do."

The good looking man stands to greet Megan.

"It looked like a special occasion. You

have my card. Why don't you give me a call?"
"Maybe I will - sometime."

The women are walking arm in arm down Michigan Avenue. The crowds on the sidewalk part to let the happy group pass.

The women continue walking, laughing and stopping to look in store windows as they go. They stop at a cross street to let an ambulance, sirens blasting, go by.

Meanwhile at *Northwestern Emergency Room Entrance*, two attendants are rushing an obviously very pregnant young woman on a stretcher out of an ambulance into the emergency room. She is screaming.

"It's coming! The baby's coming!"

Two nurses meet them and quickly wheel the patient into a cubicle. The baby comes out shrieking. The nurse puts the infant into the arms of the young woman.

"It's a girl!"

The young woman is exhausted but beaming.

"Oh, look at her! Isn't she beautiful?"

"What's her name?"

The young mother looks intently at her new baby.

"We've thought of a lot of names, but now that I've seen her, I'm going to call her Julie."

The baby is still screaming.

The voice of the ghost of Julius is heard over the crying.

Danny! What kind of a screwed up deal did you negotiate here? Danneeeeey! Where are you? There's been a terrible mistake! Dannyforgodsakes! Where the hell are you?

FAST FORWARD – FIVE YEARS

Eric and Annie got married recently. They are starry eyed in love. A pleasure to see them so happy.

Eric owns a lovely, small house in town and as soon as Annie sold her condo, she moved in.

Eric's hobby is gardening. It was a tasteful, small wedding in the back of their home. His flowers were at the height of their blooming, on a perfect day.

Champagne, delicious small sandwiches, snacks and wedding cake followed the service.

Laura was honored by being asked to be the Matron of Honor. She had been so kind and supportive of Annie.

Everyone in attendance glowed with happiness for Annie and Eric.

Megan is back in the travel business part time, as the strict rules for agencies have been relaxed. You can now run an agency from home. She does mostly high level vacation travel from her upstairs study.

She also joined a social club. They meet monthly at an exclusive restaurant and sponsor other activities, including theatre and even ski trips. She has become a good snowboarder and loves it. She is making a life for herself. She is meeting new people but not dating anyone seriously. Maybe sometime.

Laura is one of her biggest travel clients. Her divorce settlement made her a rich woman and she can travel wherever she likes.

Alex is in Law School. Megan smiles to herself when she thinks how that would have pleased her late husband, Julius.

Sally was promoted almost immediately at her new job to General Manager. They saw right away what a whiz she is.

Shelley retired so Harriet decided not to work anymore. She is pleased to be a full time cook, although as she still says, "Shelley does not make me cook."

They took many pictures of the wedding for Catherine. She is in the Peace Corps in Guatemala. In the video of the wedding, they all told her how they missed her.

Annie loves her job as a kindergarten teacher, minutes from her new home.

One day, Annie called Megan. Her small students were having an Art Show. It was a big event for them. Mothers were supplying refreshments.

"Why don't you come? You will be surprised how talented these little ones are."

"And one more thing. The school is close. Would you have some time to volunteer for a Reading Circle a couple of times a month? The kids would love it."

Megan agreed that it would be fun. She'd think about it.

But she would definitely come to the Art Show.

As she arrived in the classroom, a beautiful little girl, with long blonde braids, came right up to her.

"Are you the Megan Miss Annie talks about? She tells us funny stories about the travel agency."

"Yes, I am. What's your name?"

"Julie."

"Do you have a painting here?"

Julie takes Megan by the hand and leads her to her work. It is almost all white, with puffy clouds and some yellow streaks of sunshine.

"That is beautiful, Julie. Does it have a name?"

"It's called 'Heaven.' I think I was there once for a short time."

"Will you come to see us again?"

"I think I am going to have a Reading Circle here. Miss Annie asked me."

After a thoughtful pause, Julie wrinkles her nose, looks at Megan intently, and says –

"That would be so cool."

Julie skips off, happily.

The mothers have arrived with the cupcakes.

ABOUT THE AUTHORS

Corinne Edwards has traveled several life paths, from business owner to sales trainer, author, blogger, lecturer, media coach and TV producer.

She is the author *of A Woman Without A Man, Reflections from a Woman Alone, Low Pain Threshold, Love Waits on Welcome . . . and other Miracles, Sales, Lies and Naked Truths, Are We Spiritual Yet, When Your Husband Has Died – A Survival Guide, Love On The Rocks* and *Media Creation.*

She produced and hosted 400 shows on national cable called *Book Tours with Corinne Edwards* for *Wisdom Television.*

She can be contacted at her blog, http://www.personal-growth-with-corinne-edwards.com.

Paul Van Name is a graduate of USC Cinema and coordinated and instructed for their summer program at Universal Studios which led to his joining the staff there in their Production Department.

He has co-produced and directed more than 400 shows for Wisdom Television.

He supplemented his college costs as a feature writer for magazines and since then has written many articles on the entertainment industry.

He enjoys collecting guitars and working on vintage *Ford* automobiles.